Divine Power in Process Theism

SUNY Series in Philosophy
Robert Cummings Neville, Editor

DAVID BASINGER

Divine Power in Process Theism

A Philosophical Critique

STATE UNIVERSITY OF NEW YORK PRESS

Published by
State University of New York Press, Albany

Printed in the United States of America

For information, address State University of New York Press, State University Plaza, Albany, N.Y., 12246

Library of Congress Cataloging in Publication Data

Basinger, David.
Divine power in process theism : a philosophical critique / David Basinger.
p. cm. — (SUNY series in philosophy)
Bibilography: p.
Includes index.
ISBN 0-88706-708-5. ISBN 0-88706-709-3 (pbk.)
1. God—History of doctrines—20th century. 2. Providence and government of God—History of doctrines—20th century. 3. Process theology—History of doctrines—20th century. I. Title.
II. Series.
BT98.B33 1988 87-24080
230'.044—dc19 CIP

10 9 8 7 6 5 4 3 2 1

CONTENTS

PREFACE

This book is, as the title states, a *critique* of process theology. And I make no apology for this fact. The more closely I consider the process system, the more troubled I become. I continue to be impressed with the emphasis on the dynamic nature of the relationship between humanity and God; I continue to be impressed with the process analysis of the relationship between human freedom and evil. But it seems to me that one of process theism's key metaphysical tenets—its conceptualization of God's power—is fraught with serious semantic and logical difficulties.

What follows, however, is meant to be a constructive critique. My goal is not to convince anyone that process theism should be discarded or not taken seriously. It is, rather, to argue that certain fundamental aspects of the process system need to be rethought.

This book is the the culmination of the work of many years. But, as is often the case with projects of this sort, I needed an extended period of time free from professional responsibilities to bring the material together into its present form. Thus, I would like to thank the administration of Roberts Wesleyan College for granting me a sabbatical for this purpose. I also wish to thank Robert Neville and especially Lewis Ford for helpful comments made on earlier drafts. Finally, I would like to thank Debbie Somerville, Sharon Steinwachs, Jan Clapsaddle and Denise Horning for typing assistance.

Parts of this book have appeared elsewhere. I wish to thank the editor of *Process Studies* for permission to reprint "Human

Coercion: A Fly in the Process Ointment?" (Vol. 15, no. 3, pp. 161-171) and parts of "Divine Omnipotence: Plantinga vs. Griffin" (Vol. 11, no. 1, pp. 11-24, co-authored with Randall Basinger), the editor of the *Journal of Regilion* for permission to reprint parts of "Divine Persuasion: Could the Process God Do More?" (Vol. 64, no. 3, pp. 332-347), and the editor of the *Evangelical Journal* for permission to reprint "Process Theology and Petitionary Prayer" (Vol. 4, no. 2, pp. 70-81).

David Basinger

INTRODUCTION

If it is true that we can best assess a movement's impact by listening to its critics, then the claim that process theism has become a significant force in American theology is undeniable. For not only proponents of process thought believe that it has been "accepted by large numbers of thinkers" and, thus, "is enjoying a period of great influence in American religious studies circles."[1] Most opponents agree. One critic has recently written, for example, that while it was true a decade ago that theology was "a many-splintered thing . . .an increasingly unifying force in modern American theology is the viewpoint known as 'process theology'."[2] Another adds that it may be *the* major school of influence of our day.[3]

Introduction to Process Thought

What exactly is this new influential school of theological thought? In one sense it is part of a rich tradition. There have been a significant number of ancient and modern philosophers who have emphasized the general concept of process—Heraclitus, Darwin, Hegel and Dewey being among the most notable. That is, many otherwise divergent thinkers, both theistic and nontheistic, have argued that "becoming is more fundamental than being."[4] Moreover, even within the confines of process theology—even with respect to those who apply process categories to God and God's relationship with the world—there is much divergence. For example, thinkers such as Henri Bergson, Teilhard de Chardin and Alfred North Whitehead, who differ on many substantive metaphysical issues, have all been labeled process theists.

Our discussion will be limited to that variant of process theology which traces its basic metaphysical origins to the work of Whitehead and much of its explicitly theological framework to the interpretation of Whitehead offered by Charles Hartshorne. This Whiteheadian/Hartshornean tradition was initially championed by such individuals as Henry Nelson Wieman, Bernard Loomer and Daniel Day Williams. More recently, its best known proponents are John Cobb, Norman Pittenger, Schubert Ogden, Lewis Ford and David Griffin.[5] I have chosen to concentrate my efforts on this tradition because I believe it to be the dominant school of process theological thought today and because I agree with those who argue that this tradition, more than any other process variant, has "generated increasing interest and excitement as a philosophical basis for Christian thought."[6]

There is, not surprisingly, much significant diversity even within this camp. However, with the exception of one significant aspect of Ogden's system, the basic metaphysical tenets of this school of thought can be summarized as follows.[7]

The most basic constituents of reality are not 'things' or enduring substances. Rather, they are little droplets of experience—usually called actual entities, actual occasions or energy-events—which momentarily come into existence and then immediately perish. Each of these actual entities has a 'physical' and 'mental' component. As the entity comes into existence, the 'physical' component takes account of (prehends) two things: its past—all that has gone before it—and God's initial aim—that which God sees as the best possibility open to it, given its concrete situation. It also automatically feels some impulse to act in accordance with God's leading. However, each entity has at least some power of self-determination—the function of its 'mental' components. Thus, no entity is ever forced to do what God wants. It always has the power to choose its own subjective aim from among God's initial aim and all other real possibilities its past has made available. Once this decision is made—once the entity has unified the data from its perspective—it perishes as an experiencing subject and its experience becomes an objective part of the past for all subsequent actual entities.

Some sets of entities, however, have a unity of their own. In these societies or aggregates of entities, each entity still inherits its past from all other entities. But its inheritance from the past members of its own society is dominant. A subatomic particle such as an electron is a good example of a basic, lower-level entity of this sort. There is no enduring substance that can be identified as an electron. But there are societies of serially-ordered 'electron' entities in which each occasion largely repeats the form of the previous entity in its society. In fact, the carry-over is so great that any given electron society appears to behave as if it were a single entity. Thus, such societies or aggregates are often called *enduring individuals.*

Moreover, basic serially-ordered enduring societies of a given type normally aggregate into more complexly structured societies (enduring individuals). Societies of subatomic particles form enduring atomic individuals which, themselves, aggregate with other enduring atomic individuals to form enduring molecular individuals which in turn aggregate with other molecular individuals. In the higher-order animal realm, for example, various societies of enduring cellular individuals aggregate to form enduring multicellular animal bodies with a central nervous system. And in some such enduring individuals, the enduring nervous system gives rise to what we label as the enduring human mind or soul.

In short, in process thought,[8] the whole is truly greater than the sum of its parts. What we perceive phenomenologically as enduring individuals—for example, humans, dogs, cats, and trees—are not just bits of inanimate and animate matter in a certain configuration. Such enduring individuals are really 'societies of societies' of varying complexity, with each society retaining to some extent its own autonomous power of self-determination even as it combines with other societies of its type to create more complex societies (individuals).

However, the more complex societies in any given 'society of societies' are dominant. The enduring society we identify as the 'brain', for example, is normally dominant over the enduring societies we identify as the muscles, which in turn are dominant over the enduring societies of cells of which they are composed. This explains why enduring individuals such as dogs and humans normally appear to function as unified wholes.

Moreover, the more complex an enduring individual, the

greater the influence of its 'mental' pole—that is, the more actual options it has open to it and the more conscious it is of such options. This explains why humans behave in much more creative, unpredictable ways than do dogs, which in turn behave in much more novel ways than do rocks.

Within process thought God is not exempted from this metaphysical order. Rather, God is considered the chief exemplification of it. God, like all other enduring individuals, is an actual entity—the supreme actual entity. And, like all other actual entities, God is dipolar. God's consequent nature—analogous to the 'physical' pole in other entities—takes account of (prehends) all that happens in the world. Other actual entities are also 'aware' to some extent of all that has occurred. But God alone experiences in its fullness all that every other entity experiences. This means that although each actual entity exists only momentarily and no other actual entity experiences at any time the past in its entirety, the past is not lost. All past occasions exist eternally as a unified whole in God's consciousness. It is in this sense that God's being includes and penetrates the whole universe. Or, as Hartshorne puts it, it is in this sense that the world is God's body.[9]

God, however, also has a primordial nature—analogous to the 'mental' pole in other entities—which responds to that which God experiences. God, in this capacity, is aware of all harmonized possibilities open to the world. And given this knowledge and the knowledge of each actual entity's individual past, God continuously presents to every entity at every moment the optimum real possibilities open to it. Moreover, as was mentioned before, each actual entity feels some compulsion (lure) to act in accordance with God's will, although such persuasion never overwhelms the entity's freedom to choose otherwise.

Thus it is that, while God is not exempted from the metaphysical rules which order the process system, God is certainly thought to be the most significant individual within it. Most process theists deny that God in any sense created the process.[10] But all maintain that it is God alone who unifies this ontological process into a harmonized whole and that God certainly does exercise more influence on the direction of the process than does any other enduring individual.

Comparison With Classical Christian Theology

Such a metaphysical system, not surprisingly, creates a theology which differs significantly from classical Judeo-Christian theology, with which it is normally compared by proponents and critics alike. The most crucial difference is related to God's power. Classical Christian theism has always held that God is the all-controlling power of the universe. This has not always been interpreted as meaning that God actually does unilaterally control all states of affairs. In fact, some classical Christians believe that God seldom chooses to become unilaterally involved in earthly activities. But such theists—often called free-will theists—still uniformly agree that God *could* unilaterally control everything. The fact that God may not always choose to do so is seen (by the relevant set of classical theists) as a self-limitation—a moral choice which in no way reflects negatively on God's power.

But within the process system, the situation is quite different. God, as we have seen, continuously influences all states of affairs. But since all actual entities always possess some degree of self-determination, God could not unilaterally control anything, even if God so desired. In other words, within process thought, the fact that God does not possess all the power is not the result of a moral choice. It is a metaphysical fact over which even God has no control. Persuasive power, as opposed to coercive power, is all that is available to God.

This means, among other things, that important theological concepts such as miracle and prayer, which traditionally presupposed unilateral divine intervention, must be radically reinterpreted in process thought.

Another important difference surfaces in relation to the doctrine of creation. Classical Christian theists have always held that God created the world *ex nihilo*. Views differ significantly with respect to the means by which this was done. But such theists have always maintained that there was once a 'time' at which only God existed and that all else was created out of nothing by divine decree.

Process theists, of course, cannot agree. Since they believe that God cannot unilaterally bring about any state of affairs, they must maintain that reality has always been the result of co-creative activity—that is, they must hold that there has always been a plurality of actual creative entities. It does seem true, most admit, that there was once a time at which there were no enduring individuals other than God. All other actual occasions probably existed in a state of random, nonpurposive activity—that is, in a state of chaos. Moreover, the fact that we now have a vast array of highly complex, multistructured societies of actual entities is, they insist, a tribute to the effectiveness of God's persuasive power. God certainly has strongly influenced the outcome of the creative process as we know it to date. But God alone can guarantee nothing. God, process theists must argue, has always been dependent on the cooperation of all other self-determining entities to accomplish any creative goal.

Furthermore, just as process theists believe there was no 'beginning', they believe there will be no 'end'. Classical Christian theism has generally held that the world will reach a final and fixed state—a final eschaton. But for process theists there will never be a time at which the current 'process' will stop. There is no ultimate state of existence at which God is aiming, a state of existence in which the basic nature of reality will be eternally fixed. There can, for example, be no fixed state of heaven and hell. The universe might at some point in time arrive at a state at which all actual entities are experiencing a very high degree of harmonious, intense novelty—the highest good from the process perspective. But there is no assurance that such a state would be long lasting. A period of disharmonious triviality—the greatest evil—could quickly follow. What does in fact occur will always depend on the manner in which all other actual entities are responding to God's leading.

On many other points, process theism normally differs from at least some significant forms of classical Christian theism. For example, most classical Christians have believed Jesus Christ to be God Incarnate—that is, to be wholly human and wholly divine. For most process theists, on the other hand, a literal characterization of the Incarnation makes little sense. Jesus was, it is granted, more closely attuned to God's leading than other humans. Thus, he can in many ways rightly show us how best to love God and others. Or, as Griffin and Cobb put this point, Jesus more than any other human "was himself open to creative transformation." Hence, "insofar as we genuinely receive Jesus as the revelation of the basic truth about reality, we are more open to the divine impulses in our experience" and, accordingly, are "more apt to respond positively to [them.]"[11]

But Jesus functioned as do all other enduring individuals: he continually used his own power of self-determination to unify his past with the real options which God and the 'world' presented to him. Thus, although Jesus can be said to have *appropriated* God to a greater degree than others, he cannot be said in any literal sense to have *been* God to any greater extent than are we.[12]

The standard process treatment of the Canon is similar in nature. For many conservative Christians in the classical tradition, the Scriptures are not simply a collection of the best thoughts of humans. They are in some sense the inspired words of God, which are, as such, capable of giving us valuable information that could not be acquired through human effort alone. Process theists, of course, cannot accept a literal interpretation of this model of inspiration. They grant that the writers of Scripture may have been more attuned to God than we are and, thus, that some (or much) of what we read in the Bible might enable us to better open ourselves up to how God would have us think and act. But they must deny that the origin of Scripture breaks the metaphysical mold. All the writers of Scripture were—as are we—individuals who at every moment encountered a past, considered the real options for future activity offered by God and the world and then made a choice. Thus, there is no basis for maintaining that what we find in the Scriptures is some sort of special, direct revelation from God. And although the Scriptures are seen as significant, most process theists see no reason why the thoughts of others, past and present, cannot have equal spiritual value.

Finally, to cite one last example, many classical Christians have thought it important to hold that God is omniscient in the sense that all that has occurred, is occurring or will occur (including what we will freely choose to do) is open to the divine vision. But process theists, not surprisingly, deny that God possesses such insight. God does, they acknowledge, know all that has occurred. However, since all reality is co-creative—since every droplet of experience includes the self-determination of entities other than

God—God cannot know in advance what the choices of any entity will be. God can, of course, accurately predict what will occur to a greater degree than we. But no certain knowledge of the future is possible even for God, it is argued, for there is presently nothing certain about the future for God to know.

Basis for Its Popularity

Why is it that this relatively young, nontraditional school of thought has gained such prominence? Some agree with Norman Pittenger that it is primarily because process theism appears to offer contemporary thinkers a way out of the antimetaphysical morass in which theology has been entrapped without making the overly grandiose traditional metaphysical claim that it can "explain or describe the totality of things." Process theology, they grant, does reply heavily on philosophical conceptuality. But it seems to do so in what "might be called metaphysics 'in a new mode', beginning as it does with concrete human experience and the world in which the experience is set—and never claiming to be more than a suitable and useful 'version of reality', to use Whitehead's own phrase for his philosophical conclusions."[13]

Others feel that the primary appeal of process thought is its view of God. Only from a process perspective, they maintain, can we coherently conceive of a God who truly feels with us and is there to help us in our daily struggles. And only from this perspective can we preserve God's moral integrity in the face of evil.

Still others emphasize the fact that process thought seemingly provides a needed cultural emphasis on "feeling, community, and intimacy without the irresponsibility that accompanies this emphasis in the counterculture" or the fact that process thought seemingly "answers the need for an ecologically sound approach to the universe."[14] And all agree that process theism is appealing in part because it appears to have "made peace with modern science" to a greater degree than any of its competitors.[15]

Some critics, however, envision less noble motives. One states, for example, that a major factor in the growth of process thought may simply be "the desire for a bakery-fresh made-in-America theology."[16] Another critic goes so far as to say that the real appeal of process thought lies in the fact that it "allows the modern thinker [as opposed to a sovereign God] to be in charge of things."[17]

Categorization of Critiques

Whatever the actual appeal (or appeals) might be, the fact remains that process theism is a major force to be reckoned with in contemporary theological studies. As such, it has generated a great deal of critical discussion. Such critiques, I believe, are best divided into four basic categories.

First, there are what I shall call theological attacks on process thought. I label them 'theological' because in all such critiques it is argued that certain propositions affirmed by process theists should be considered false because they are incompatible with other theological propositions known to be true on independent grounds.

Consider, for example, the following assessment of process thought by F. Duane Lindsey:

> Process theology falls short of being Christian in many areas. The rejection of creation in favor of a system which needs an eternal universe, the rejection of the finality of Christianity, the rejection of total depravity and biblical morality, and the rejection of direct, supernatural revelation are a few examples of the many departures of process theology from biblical Christianity.[18]

Others echo the same theme. Bruce Demarest's "primary criticism of process theology is that its god is not the God of the Bible."[19] Clark Pinnock tells us that "no one with a high view of the Bible is going to be able to accept [the process model of God].... The ontological transcendence of God is essential if we are to maintain the biblical picture of God's freedom and redemptive activity."[20]

Such criticisms must be clearly distinguished from those which simply comment upon the relationship between process theism and classical Christian thought. They must be distinguished, for example, from Michael Peterson's claim that "however tantalizing it may be to some contemporary thinkers, the wedding [of process thought and classical Christianity] cannot be successfully consummated."[21] Comments of this latter sort are not really criticisms at all. They make only a descriptive claim: that process theism is incompatible with classical Christian thought. And this is something with which the vast majority of process thinkers will agree. In fact, it is a claim they often make themselves.

Critics such as Lindsey, Demarest and Pinnock, on the other hand, are not simply giving us descriptive information. They are not simply describing *differences* between process thought and its competitors. Their comments are normative in nature. They are claiming that because certain process beliefs differ from what they consider orthodox, such beliefs *ought to* be rejected.

Is this type of normative criticism valid? There is one sense in which I believe it is. Some classical Christians may have desired to embrace certain aspects of process thought without being fully aware of the problematic implications of attempting such a synthesis. And it seems to me that it is perfectly valid for classical critics to point this out to their classical friends. Or, to state the point differently, it seems to me that to the extent to which critics such as Lindsey are directing their remarks to other classical Christian theists—individuals who already affirm the 'orthodox' truths in question—their normative attacks are justifiable.

It is not always clear, however, that such critics actually do mean to direct their remarks solely to fellow classical Christians. At times it appears that they have a wider audience in mind—for example, all sincere Christian theists. But to the extent this is true, their theological critiques seem to me to be question-begging. The *descriptive* claim that the concept of God affirmed by process theists differs from that affirmed by classical theists still stands. But the *normative* claim that the classical concept is the 'right' one need not be acknowledged by anyone who does not already share the classical assumptions on which this claim is based.

In other words, theological criticisms of the type under consideration are of significant, but limited, value. They do legitimately serve to clarify the thinking of some classical Christians. But once they are directed to the religious community at large, their only value is descriptive: to point out that classical theism and process theism are on some points incompatible. And this is hardly news to anyone.

A second basic type of criticism is primarily concerned with methodological issues. That is, a number of critics contend that process theism's approach to theological issues is seriously flawed.

One such critic complains that process thought "is based upon speculation, not actual experience."[22] But such a charge is dubious. Process theism is, of course, a speculative metaphysical perspective. However, so are all of its theological competitors, including classical Christian theism. Moreover, proponents of all such perspectives, process theism included, maintain that they are "based upon" actual experience in the sense that they best organize and explain it. In fact, it appears that process theism is actually "based upon" experience to a greater degree than classical Christianity, which gives more consideration to propositional revelation.

Another critic, David Burrell, doubts whether the process methodology can rightly be called theological at all. For "one of the demands of an 'adequate theological conceptuality'," he tells us, "has always been to illuminate and recover the tradition." And process theology tends to "neglect this dialectical exercise," accepting instead "consistency with Whiteheadian philosophy as the principal criterion."[23]

However, this criticism also seems misguided. It is certainly true that any 'new theology' which claims to be a variant of some specific theological tradition must "illuminate and recover" that tradition. But process theology has never claimed to be a variant of the classical theology Burrell affirms. Just the opposite is true. Hence, process thinkers are not obligated to concern themselves with the type of 'recovery' task Burrell envisions. All that such thinkers are required to do—to the extent they call themselves Christian—is to explain how traditional Christian concepts such as sin, salvation, grace and atonement are to be interpreted in the process system. And this requirement they clearly meet.

Still another methodological critic has argued that process theologians do not take Scripture seriously. "When Scripture conflicts with [process] beliefs, it is conveniently ignored or casually discarded."[24] However, there appears to be little objective basis for such a claim. Process theists do approach Scripture differently than do many (especially conservative) classical

Christians. However, it in no sense follows from this fact that process theists are not serious about biblical studies. In fact, the increasing number of discussions of biblical issues written from a process perspective would tend to support the claim that process biblicists are serious indeed.

The majority of methodological criticisms, however, attack what is seen as an unjustifiable emphasis on human reason. Royce Gruenler's response to Hartshorne's perceived rejection of the 'theory of infallible revelation' is a good illustration:

> This rejection of God's self-disclosure in sacred Scripture... leads to a confusion of deity and humanity, for now human reason becomes the final arbiter of what God may be conceived to be and of his worthiness to be worshipped. The first and last court of appeal is the enlightened person who numbers himself among those men of the highest integrity and wisdom who have attempted to worship the objective God, not our forefathers' doctrines about him. This is anthropocidy, a defense of human autonomy and reason against the claims of biblical revelation.[25]

Since this type of methodological criticism is quite similar to the theological critiques discussed earlier, an analogous assessment can be made. To the extent to which critics such as Gruenler are descriptively pointing out meaningful methodological differences between process thought and their own, what they say is correct. Moreover, to the extent to which they are talking to individuals who already hold similar theological beliefs, they can justifiably argue that the process methodology should be rejected. But to the extent to which they are offering this negative normative assessment to the general intellectual community, their criticisms strike me as weak. If the classical Christian emphasis on revelation and faith (or the neo-orthodox emphasis on antirationalism) is in fact methodologically superior to the process emphasis on reason, then we must have arguments to this end which are not based on premises which already presuppose that which is to be proved. And such arguments I have not yet seen. (In fact, it seems to me that it would be much easier to establish the opposite: that all theologies are most fundamentally based on 'human reason'.)

A third basic type of criticism can best be labeled 'evidential' or 'factual'. The critics in this category differ from those offering theological critiques in that they are not content just to argue that certain process claims must be rejected because they are incompatible with certain truths which can be established on independent grounds. They desire, rather, to attack specific process claims, themselves, by arguing that compelling evidence shows such claims to be false.

One common criticism of this sort is leveled against the standard process characterization of the classical Christian God. According to most process thinkers, the classical "God's influence upon the world is in no way conditioned by divine responsiveness to [the] unforeseen, self-determining activities of us wordly beings." The classical God is an "unchangeable, passionless, absolute" being who is "wholly independent of [its creation]."[26]

But such a characterization, many argue, is actually a distorted caricature. Langdon Gilkey, for example, tells us that "what process philosophers of religion call 'classical theism' is a strange hodgepodge that bears little historical scrutiny; and, as philosophers are wont to do, they seem to think that it has been scholastic *philosophy* that dominated the religion and piety of almost all of western Christendom until finally a new philosophy appeared in Whitehead."[27]

To some extent, this criticism is justified. Some process theists have been guilty of wrongly assuming that all variations of classical Christian thought are governed by the Aristotelian view of immutability. But most process theists have not meant their characterization of the God of classical theism to be seen as descriptive. That is, their claim is not that most classical Christians *do* in fact believe their God to be a totally passionless, unresponsive being who is never affected by earthly affairs. Their argument, rather, is that this is what classical Christians *should* believe if they really do affirm the classical doctrines of divine immutability and divine sovereignty.

Accordingly, to attack the process characterization of the classical Christian God, the classical theist must do more than simply tell us that this characterization does not accurately describe his or her actual beliefs. Most process theists already know this. The classical theist must either deny that the traditional doctrines of sovereignty and immutability actually need to be affirmed or argue that once these traditional doctrines are properly explicated, the implications drawn by process theists do not follow. Some classical theists have in fact done just that (and I believe successfully).[28] But the majority of classical critics still seem confused on this point.

Another popular set of evidential attacks is leveled against the basic process metaphysic itself. Many such critics challenge the process contention that reality is, in its most ultimate sense, something best labeled 'creativity' and not 'substance'. Illtyd Trethowan, for instance, finds the process contention that "the source of all things is something called 'creativity'" to be "an implausible metaphysical theory."[29] And, according to Burrell, most metaphysicians agree.[30]

Many others, such as Gruenler, see an even more serious "flaw at the very core of process metaphysics," namely that it "is not really compatible with modern relativity theory"—that is, it is not compatible with modern views of space and time.[31]

Such fundamental metaphysical criticisms seem to me to be significant challenges worthy of serious consideration by anyone interested in assessing process thought. And I have not personally found many of the process responses convincing. But ultimate metaphysical schemes are very resilient; they usually can be adjusted to subsume even the most seemingly recalcitrant data. Moreover, I know of no way to adjudicate objectively between self-consistent, comprehensive conceptual schemes. Thus, it seems to me that although evidential attacks upon the basic process metaphysic may well continue to necessitate some revision, no such attack will offer a 'knock-out blow'.

However, by far the most common type of evidential criticism is leveled against the theological adequacy of the God of process theism. Clark Pinnock speaks for many when he argues that, although process theists mount

> an impressive argument for the way a process deity can supply a firm basis for our confidence in the worthwhileness of our existence, I think many people will feel that a godling of this small proportion is not big enough to satisfy their religious needs. They would naturally feel that a God who is neither creator or [sic] redeemer of the world in any strong sense does

> not deserve to be called God, and is vastly inferior to the God of the Bible.[32]

Michael Peterson goes even further. The values and methods of the God of process theism, he believes, "are not fundamentally moral, but nonmoral or perhaps immoral." For, rather than communicating "a clear message to his creatures 'from outside' themselves," God only "nudges them 'from deep within'." Thus, since "perfect moral goodness is a necessary condition of worshipworthiness," the God of process theism is not worthy of worship.[33]

Not surprisingly, process theists see things differently. They agree that a God who is worthy of worship must both satisfy our religious needs and be perfectly good. But they maintain that only the God of process theism meets these requirements. The powerful, independent God of classical Christian theism, they grant, might justifiably be viewed as a convenient wish-fulfiller. But such a being cannot justifiably be viewed as a caring friend worthy of our loving respect. Moreover, they emphatically continue, given the amount of unnecessary evil we experience, only a God who could not do more to remove it can be considered perfectly good.[34]

Which camp is correct? What type of 'God' is truly worthy of worship? It seems to me that this is a question to which there is no objective answer. We might be able to establish that any divine being within a Christian context would have to possess certain attributes—for example, moral perfection and a loving attitude. And we might even be able to demonstrate that the majority of Christian theists do at this point in time believe that the God of classical Christianity exemplifies such attributes to a greater degree than does the God of process theism or vice versa. But, ultimately, a person's perspective on the question of theological adequacy will be derived from his or her basic axiological framework—that is, from the manner in which he or she value-structures reality. And I can conceive of no objective manner in which it can be established that the basic axiological framework of classical Christian theism is any more or less 'accurate' than its process counterpart.

This brings us, finally, to the fourth basic type of criticism of process thought: the philosophical (logical) critique. Such critiques are not primarily concerned with the orthodoxy, adequacy or accuracy of process claims. Nor are they concerned with the methodology by which such claims are generated. Such critiques, rather, are primarily concerned with questions of logical consistency.

Some of these philosophical critiques are responses to attempts by process theists to demonstrate the incoherence of classical theism. For instance, Ogden has claimed that classical theists contradict themselves when they claim both that God freely creates a contingent world and that "God's act of creation is one with his own eternal essence, which is in every respect necessary," for if we give "full weight to both of [these] assertions, we at once find ourselves in the hopeless contradiction of a wholly necessary creation of a wholly contingent world."[35] But critics such as Robert Neville argue that "it is not at all contradictory to say that the world is wholly contingent in the sense that it needs a cause other than itself in order to exist at all, and that God the cause necessarily produces its effect. This is only to say that without the cause the effect would not exist, but that with the cause it must exist."[36]

Other philosophical critiques attack the process system directly, claiming either that basic tenets within the system, itself, are self-contradictory or that implications commonly drawn from such tenets do not actually follow. For instance, process theists claim that since "to be actual is to be in process" and to be in process is to be engaged in self-determining activity, God cannot know the future in advance. For there is currently nothing actual about the future for God to know.[37] But William Craig has recently argued that it is possible to affirm the process perspective on self-determinism without denying divine foreknowledge.[38]

Or, to cite another example, process theists hold that although God and the world are attuned to each other so as to make up a single unified system, the activity of neither is totally dependent on the other. But critics such as Norris Clarke question the intelligibility of this process tenet. How, they ask rhetorically, "can diversity account for sameness, multiplicity for unity, when diversity and multiplicity by their very definition entail otherness, not sameness? How can we speak of one world when there is only multiplicity and no primal unity? . . . [T]here can only be otherness in such a world."[39]

Such philosophical critiques have, in principle, an inherent advantage over the other three types of criticisms mentioned. When we attempt to determine the orthodoxy, adequacy or accuracy of certain process tenets, we are essentially attempting to determine what is 'true'. And, as we have seen, this is no easy task, for what one considers to be true is often relative to one's basic nondemonstrable metaphysical assumptions. But the philosophical critiques in question are not concerned with the actual truth or falsity of process claims. Their task is more limited: to determine whether what process theists say is self-consistent. And the consistency of a proposition (or set of propositions), all will agree, is, in principle, much easier to assess than its truth or falsity.

In practice, however, we must be cautious when considering alleged philosophical critiques of process thought. First, what may appear to be a logical problem is sometimes based on a misreading of process thought. Gruenler's assessment of the following passage from one of David Griffin's books offers us a good illustration.

> [Creativity] is inherent in actuality. . . .This does not mean that creatures derive their creative power from themselves, or that they are not dependent upon God for their existence. But it does mean that to be an actuality is to exercise creativity, and that there is necessarily a realm of finite actualities with creativity of their own.[40]

According to Gruenler, there is an inconsistency in this passage. "How could creatures derive their power not from themselves but from God and at the same time comprise a realm of finite actualities with creativity of their own *necessarily*? The two statements are logically contradictory."[41]

But Griffin never said that creatures derive their *creative power* from God, as Gruenler maintains. Griffin says rather that they are not totally independent of God for their *existence* (by which he means that all creatures must always consider God's initial aim when freely choosing how to unify (create) their own experience). And this is a radically different claim. In fact, Griffin explicitly says in the same context from which Gruenler quotes that "the fact that the world's actual entities have creature power is... beyond all volition, even God's."[42]

Second, we must not confuse the acknowledged fact that specific process theists hold certain beliefs which are incompatible with those held by other process theists with the claim that the process system is, itself, self-contradictory. All theological systems, classical Christian theism included, have proponents who affirm certain tenets which are incompatible with those held by other proponents. To mount a successful philosophical attack on process theism (or any other theological system), one must either demonstrate that the basic, commonly accepted tenets are self-contradictory or demonstrate that a specific proponent's version is, itself, inconsistent.

Finally, and most importantly, it is not always easy to determine whether a given statement (or set of statements) is, in fact, self-consistent. Take, for example, the age-old question of whether divine foreknowledge and human freedom are compatible. Few claim that there is an immediate and obvious contradiction in this case. But many (including most process theists) have argued that once we draw out the implications of these concepts, a contradiction appears. Specifically, they maintain that if God has always infallibly known that we will perform certain actions, then we have no choice but to do so, and that, if this is so, it cannot be said that we are performing the actions freely. However, many others (including many critics of process thought) disagree. They point out that we do not perform actions *because* God knows we will do so; rather God's knowledge of what we will do *is based* on that which will be done. Thus, it is their contention that no incompatibility exists.

In short, we must keep in mind that although consistency itself is a somewhat objective concept, its applicability to any specific aspect of the process system may remain quite subjective—that is, may remain a matter of perspective.

Summarization of Chapter Context

This book is primarily a philosophical discussion. I will, at times, attempt to determine the truth or falsity of claims made by process theists and their critics. However, my primary goal will be to assess the self-consistency of the process system. More specifically, my discussion will center around one basic component in the process system: the process conception of divine power. I have not centered on this aspect of process thought because I believe it to be the only important concept which can be profitably subjected to philosophical analysis. The process commitment to divine contingency is also of great significance. However, this aspect of process thought has already been discussed in detail.[43] Moreover, I believe the process conception of divine power to be the most fundamental and important component in the process system. Process perspectives on such important theological concepts as miracle, prayer, guidance, grace, salvation, Christ, revelation and evil all flow directly from the process understanding of how much power God wields vis-à-vis the world.

Moreover, this book is primarily a critique. This should not be taken to mean that I am an ardent opponent of process thought. I am basically in agreement with the process methodology. I, too, believe that the basic task of theology is to build an existentially and intellectually satisfying metaphysical framework to organize and explain human experience. I am also in agreement with much of what process theists have to say about evil, human freedom and divine immanence. However, I do believe that the process conception of divine power is inherently flawed and, thus, that much of theological significance within the process system needs to be rethought.

In Chapter I, I assess the key premise in the process theists's understanding of God's power: the contention that God *cannot* unilaterally control any actual state of affairs.[44] Process theists, as I have already mentioned, are not the only ones who challenge the claim that God unilaterally intervenes in earthly affairs on a continuous basis. Many classical free will Christians also maintain that God seldom intervenes in this manner. But, for them, nonintervention is the result of divine self-limitation. That is, for classical free will theists, God's forfeiture of unilateral control (to whatever extent it is forfeited) is a *moral* choice.

Most process theists, on the other hand, do not believe that God has *chosen* not to control unilaterally earthly affairs—that is, divine noncoercion is not believed to be the result of a moral decision. It is viewed, rather, as a metaphysical necessity over which not even God has control. God could not coerce even if God wanted to.

I argue, however, that this fundamental process claim is dubious. Process theists, I maintain, have not given us convincing reasons for believing that a being who possesses the acknowledged attributes of the God of process theism could not at times coerce other beings in the sense in which we normally use the term—that is, could not unilaterally restrict the ability of other beings to act in accordance with their desires. If I am correct, then process theism essentially collapses into a form of classical free will Christianity in relation to most significant theological issues. And if this is so, then process thought can be considered no more adequate (or less problematic) than this classical variant, as many process theists strongly contend.

Let us assume for the sake of argument, however, that God cannot coerce in any sense. It still remains the case that we as humans can coerce in the important sense just mentioned. We can unilaterally restrict the ability of others to act in accordance with their desires. Hitler certainly did so when he placed the Jews in concentration camps. Parents do so when they finally pick up their recalcitrant children and make them go to bed. And government officials certainly act coercively in this sense when they refuse to give their citizenry any input into the formulation of the laws by which they are governed.

Can process theists ever condone the use of such coercive power? Or, to state the question a bit more formally: When, if ever, can the process theist justifiably condone the unilateral restriction of someone's self-determination?

In Chapter II, I argue that we discover fundamental consistency problems in process thought when we attempt to answer this question. If the God of process theism could in fact coerce but has chosen not to—that is, if noncoercion were a moral decision —then process theists would have a sound moral basis for determining the types of power we as humans can justifiably utilize. However, process theism explicitly claims that God cannot coerce. And it in no sense necessarily follows from this metaphysical fact that the use of coercive power, where possible, is or is not morally superior to the use of noncoercive power. Hence, since process theists, like their classical counterparts, believe that the practice of one's faith in the actual world must ultimately find its basis in one's doctrine of God, the fundamental question becomes: Would the God of process theism occasionally coerce in the sense in question if this were an option?

Unfortunately, in whatever manner process theists attempt to respond to this question, serious tensions develop. If they maintain that God would not coerce even if this were possible, they retain a strong basis for claiming that persuasion is morally (and even practically) superior to coercion. But it is then difficult to see how process theists can justifiably maintain (as do almost all leading process theists) that God wants us as humans to use coercive power at times or how they can justifiably criticize the God of classical free will theism for not coercing more often. On the other hand, if process theists decide that God would coerce at times if this were possible, they do establish a sound basis for the human use of coercion in some cases. But they must then discard the common process contention that coercion is morally "incompatible with divine perfection" and the claim that persuasion is always the greatest of all powers, the only one "capable of any worthwhile result."[45] Furthermore, they must acknowledge that humans possess a 'desirable' form of power God simply does not possess. Something, it appears, must give.

In Chapter III, I argue that ambiguities and consistency problems also permeate the process discussion of the problem of evil. As we have seen, process theists believe their theodicy to be superior to those theodicies found in classical theism. For while classical theists, it is argued, cannot explain why their God, who can unilaterally coerce, has not used this power to eliminate more evil, the God of process theism faces no such challenge since this being cannot coerce. In other words, process theists believe that only their view of God preserves God's moral integrity in the face of evil.

In response, I first challenge the contention that a God who could unilaterally remove more evil would be morally bound to do so. Classical free will Christians, I argue, can give a self-consistent account as to why, in a world containing meaningful human freedom, a perfectly good God would not 'do more' even though this being has the 'strength' to do so, an account which they need not grant is less plausible than that offered by process theism. I also point out the basic inconsistency between process theism's critique of classical theodicies and its moral assessment of persuasive power. As I have already mentioned, most process theists clearly hold that persuasive power is both morally and efficaciously superior to coercive power. But if process theists really believe this, how then can they also contend that the classical free will theodicy is inadequate because a morally perfect being with coercive capabilities would intervene more than the classical God has done?

In Chapter IV, I discuss the eschatological question of whether good will ultimately triumph over evil in the process system. Not surprisingly, process theists think so. They grant that since God cannot unilaterally intervene in earthly affairs and since there is no ultimate end to the evolutionary process in which we find ourselves, such 'triumph' cannot be of the same type as that claimed in classical Christian thought. God cannot guarantee that good will ultimately triumph over evil on the earthly stage. And there cannot be a separate, heavenly realm in which the "scales are ultimately balanced."

But the ultimate evil, process theists tell us, is perpetual perishing—the seeming fact that, although there is much enjoyment and intrinsic value in our present experiences, all that we accomplish and enjoy will pass into oblivion. And God does clearly triumph over this evil, we are told. God not only retains all experiences eternally; God ultimately reconciles all disharmonious aspects of reality into a harmonious whole. Moreover, to the extent we align ourselves with God's purposes, we, too, can personally experience this form of triumph.

I argue, however, that while this model of triumph is self-consistent, there is little reason to believe it to be superior to that offered by classical Christian theism. Moreover, this process vision of hope seems to undercut the standard process critique of the classical free will response to evil in that such a vision radically downplays the significance of the mental and physical anguish we experience—the very type of evil which must be emphasized to make the process critique effective.

In Chapter V, I turn my attention to the process perspective on another important theological concept: petitionary prayer. All Christian traditions, including process theism, emphasize the importance of prayer. Moreover, within almost all such traditions it is quite clearly held, to use the words of David Mason, that believers "are to ask God for things" and that God "hears, is affected by our importunities, and responds adequately to them."[46] Within certain forms of classical Christianity this is often taken to mean that God at times unilaterally intervenes in earthly affairs primarily because of human requests. God, for example, is sometimes said to heal, give guidance or control the physical environment primarily in response to our petitions.

But process theists, as we have seen, deny that God can unilaterally bring about any state of affairs. Moreover, they believe that at every moment God is already doing all that can be done to maximize the well-being of every entity. Thus, it might appear that petitionary prayer would be a vacuous concept within process thought. What sense could it make to petition a being who cannot become more involved than it already is?

Some process theists, however, deny that petitionary prayer is a meaningless concept. They argue instead that at least one common type of petitionary prayer—intercessory prayer for others—is indeed efficacious both in the lives of the petitioners and in the lives of those for whom the petitions are offered. I argue, however, that all such attempts to salvage a meaningful sense of petitionary prayer ultimately fail. Process theists do have a sound basis for regularly engaging in prayer. But given the manner in which process theism must define 'petitionary prayer' to make it efficacious—as an activity in which we generate efficacious conscious thoughts by talking with God about things—it seems doubtful that petitionary prayer, as opposed to other methods of producing conscious thoughts—for example, by talking with friends—is the best way to generate such efficacy. Moreover, their use of classical petitionary language blurs what process theists see as the important distinction between their view of divine power and those views held by classical theists. Accordingly, it seems to me that it would be best (most consistent with their basic tenets) for process theists to disavow petitionary prayer altogether.

Chapter VI is a discussion of spiritual discernment. Christians do not only believe it is important to share their thoughts with God in prayer. They also want God to share information with them. That is, they want to know God's will. But to what extent is it possible for believers to discern God's will? I argue that although such discernment is by its very nature difficult for any Christian, process theists encounter special problems. To the extent that they maintain that God's leading comes from within—is a subjective experience—process theists, like all other 'subjectivists', must grapple with an obvious question: How does one know the 'feeling' in question is really from God? Most classical Christians believe that direct conscious divine input is possible and that, when actually occurring, is self-authenticating. Process theists, however, deny that direct conscious communication with God is open to all. God can 'speak' directly only to our subconscious, and this 'message' rarely, if ever, presents itself to the consciousness intact. Thus, process theists can, in principle, have only limited confidence in subjective leading.

On the other hand, to the extent process theists attempt to deduce God's specific will from their doctrine of God, they, like all other 'rationalists', face the problem of finite perspective—the problem of attempting to make such deductions without knowledge of all the relevant factors. But process theists face an additional problem. While classical Christians assume that the betterment of humanity is God's ultimate creative ideal and, thus, is the principle on which all human activity must ultimately be grounded, process theism does not give humanity this special status. Accordingly, process theists must grapple not only with determining how specific courses of action will impact humanity. They must also grapple with the status of humanity, itself, vis-à-vis God's creative goals.

Such difficulties, I conclude, should lead process theists to be very reluctant to endorse strongly any specific sense of leading as the one God actually sanctions.

In closing, two comments are necessary. First, it is important that I explicitly reemphasize why I have been comparing, and will continue to compare, process theism primarily with classical Judeo-Christian thought of an Augustinian/Thomistic variety. It is not because I believe this variant of classical theism to be more significant than its non-Christian or mystical Christian counterparts. It is rather that rationalistic Christian theism is the type of classical theism with which process theists normally compare themselves. Hence, since this book is an attempt to assess the consistency of claims made by process thinkers, I, too, have decided to narrow my discussion of classical thought in a similar manner. (Those who wish to assess the relationship between process thought and other world religions are directed to Neville's *Creativity and God*.[47])

Second, let me emphasize that what follows is meant to be a constructive critique. I do believe there to be some fundamental confusions in the process understanding of God's power. But I agree with David Burrell that "in philosophical theology significant mistakes may indeed advance the discussion—significantly."[48]

Chapter I

DIVINE PERSUASION

COULD THE GOD OF PROCESS THEISM DO MORE?

One of the most significant theological claims made by process theists[1] is that their understanding of the relationship between God and the world is more accurate and satisfying than that found in classical Christian theism. The God of classical theism, we are told, possesses and exercises coercive power. That is, God can and does at times force us to act in accordance with the divine will. But to conceive of God in this manner, it is argued, gives us no adequate explanation for moral evil and does not allow us to assume that anyone other than God possesses meaningful freedom or self-determination. The God of process theism, on the other hand, is said never to coerce in this sense. God never forces us to act in accordance with the divine will. God attempts to persuade us to do only that which is best. And to conceive of God in this manner, process theists conclude, allows us to take both evil and freedom seriously.

The purpose of this chapter is to assess the fundamental contention on which this comparison rests: the claim that the God of process theism *never* coerces. I shall argue that while such a being may choose never to coerce, process theists have given us no good reason to believe that their God could not coerce, and thus no good reason to believe that their 'persuasive' God is significantly different than the 'coercive' God of some forms of classical Christian theism (hereafter referred to as classical theism).[2]

Process Perspective on Divine Persuasion

What exactly do process theists mean when they say that God never coerces? It is sometimes thought to mean that God never unilaterally brings about any state of affairs.[3] But this is inaccurate. According to process thought, to be persuaded or lured by God is to have both a cognitive and an affective experience. It is cognitive in the sense that God's lure "provides" or "furnishes" us at each moment with God's understanding of that which would be best for us to actualize.[4] And such luring is affective in that it is "felt knowledge, not mere conceptualization."[5] That is, it is an impulse which draws us "toward an ideal in some tension with our other urges and desires."[6] It is not always clear exactly how strong process theists believe this cognitive/affective lure to be. But they agree that such divine persuasion "is not ineffective."[7]

Or, to state this point differently, although it may be that entities differ in their awareness of and openness to divine persuasion, no entity, according to process thought, can avoid such persuasion entirely. Each automatically becomes aware of God's initial aim at each moment and feels some compulsion to actualize it. But, of course, for God to bring it about unilaterally that other entities have such cognitive/affective experiences is for God to bring about unilaterally certain states of affairs. In short, the God of process theism is coercive in this sense.

In what sense then is it that God can properly be said not to coerce? The answer is related to the perceived efficacy or strength of the divine lure. The crucial question, as process theists see it, is not whether God unilaterally lures each entity but whether such luring ever insures (unilaterally brings it about) that God's ideal aim—God's understanding of what would be best for the entity in question—is actualized. And to this question, process theists respond with an emphatic no. Lewis Ford, for example, acknowledges that each entity must consider God's ideal. But such luring, he adds, "is effective in determining the outcome only to the extent that the process appropriates and reaffirms for itself the aims envisioned in the persuasion."[8] John Cobb and David Griffin agree. In every case, they point out, "the subject may choose to actualize (God's) initial aim; but it may also choose from among the other real possibilities open to it."[9]

In short, when process theists claim that God is only persuasive, they do not (or ought not) mean that God never unilaterally brings about anything. What they really mean is that God never brings it about unilaterally that other entities must act in accordance with the divine will.

Critique of the Process Perspective

Why exactly is it that the God of process theism never coerces in this sense? Is it that God has the capacity to coerce other entities but has chosen not to do so? That is, is noncoercion a self-limitation? Or is it that God does not have the capacity to coerce other actual entities? That is, is it the case that God could not coerce other actual entities even if this were a desired end?

Occasionally, it appears as if some process theists view divine noncoercion as a self-limitation.[10] But, in fact, the vast majority of process theists unambiguously maintain that coercion is something of which God is not capable. That is, they agree with Griffin that divine noncoercion "is not due to a decision on God's part which *could* be revoked from time to time."[11] But why should we assume that God is thus limited? Why should we believe that God could not even occasionally coerce other entities if this were something God desired to do?

Griffin offers us one popular response. To affirm that God could coerce (unilaterally control the actions of) another entity, he argues, is to affirm that "it is possible for one actual being's condition to be completely determined by a being or beings other than itself."[12] However, he continues, actual entities can be completely determined only if they are "totally devoid of all power—power to determine themselves, even partially, and power to determine others, even partially."[13] But "talk of powerless actualities is finally meaningless," we are told, "since it cannot be given any experiential basis"—that is, since we "know it is possible for an actuality to have power" but have no "direct knowledge that (powerless) entities are possible."[14] Thus, he concludes, it is necessarily the case that no entity, including God, can unilaterally control other entities.

If Griffin is correct, then we should obviously not be able to cite any examples from human experience in which one person is unilaterally controlled by another. But such control does appear to exist. Let us consider the case of a parent who, after trying unsuccessfully to convince a child to go to bed, finally picks up the child and takes him or her into the bedroom. Or let us consider the case of a parent who finally ends a fight between siblings by forcibly separating the children. Do we not here have two common cases in which one entity (a parent) unilaterally controls the behavior of another entity (a child)?

Many process theists will maintain that we do not. They will grant that parents do at times control their children's behavior. But in all such cases they will attempt to demonstrate that the children retain some power of self-determination. They might argue, for example, that, even when a parent can bring it about that a child goes to bed or stops fighting, the child retains the power to resist physically or the power to desire not to act as the parent wishes or the power to plan revenge. Moreover, they agree with Griffin that a person is being totally controlled only if she or he has no power of self-determination. Thus, they will conclude that parents never really control their children and, accordingly, that parental control is not a valid counter-example to the claim that one person can never coerce another.

This line of reasoning, however, is problematic. It may well be that no being can unilaterally control another in the sense that the former can cause the latter to be devoid of all power of self-determination. But it is not with this form of coercion that we as humans are primarily concerned. For example, when we as members of society commission our police force to protect us from thieves and rapists, we are not asking (and may not even be desiring) that such felons be made devoid of all power of self-determination. We only want to insure that such individuals do not have the power to act out certain antisocial desires. In a similar fashion, those who contend that God ought to do more to curb the moral evil in the world are not generally arguing that an all-powerful, perfectly good being should bring it about that those who desire to perform evil acts are devoid of all power of self-determination. They are arguing that God ought to bring it about unilaterally that potential evildoers are unable to act out certain antisocial, dehumanizing desires.

Accordingly, for the process theist to argue that unilateral behavioral control is not really coercion unless such control also causes the being in question to be devoid of all power of self-determination is in a very real sense for the process theist to 'win the battle but lose the war'. To define coercion in this fashion may allow the process theist to claim that God never coerces. But if it does not follow from the fact that God cannot coerce in this sense that God also cannot unilaterally control the behavior of other entities, then the victory is only verbal. For if a being—a parent or God—can control the behavior of another being without coercing it (in Griffin's sense), then Griffin's argument is irrelevant to the type of unilateral control with which we are normally concerned.

Moreover, it is not clear that humans cannot in fact be coerced in the strong sense intended by process theists like Griffin. It may be true in the two examples cited previously that the children retained some meaningful sense of self-determination. But let us consider the unfortunate case of the parent who kills his or her child in anger or frustration. The parent in this situation is not simply controlling one aspect of a self-determining individual's behavior. The parent is unilaterally bringing it about that the child is devoid of the "power to determine (itself), even partially and (the) power to determine others even partially."

In response, it might be argued that a parent who kills his or her child is not unilaterally controlling the actions of an entity but only bringing it about unilaterally that an entity can perform no action at all and that it is only the former which Griffin argues is true coercion. But this again is at best a verbal victory. Given the type of coercion with which we are normally concerned, it is truly coercive for one being to bring it about unilaterally that another being no longer possesses the ability to act at all. For such activity does unilaterally determine another being's behavior.

There is, however, another way in which the proponent of Griffin's argument might respond to examples of seemingly unilateral parental control (in moderate or extreme forms). For process theism, what we normally identify as a human is really a higher-order society of enduring actual entities, each of which is being lured by God in a specific and individual (although coordinated) manner. It might be argued, accordingly, that although one higher-order society of actual entities (a parent) can at times unilaterally control the spatio-temporal characteristics of other higher-order socieites (children), no such society can, itself, control unilaterally the self-determined activity of each specific actual entity of which another higher-order society is composed.

But again problems arise. Even if it is true in some meaningful sense that a given society of entities can be coerced while some of its members remain free, we as humans are primarily interested in the behavior of other humans. Thus, the crucial question remains. Can God, as a specific actual entity, unilaterally control the behavior of humans?[15]

Humans, it might be granted in response, do unilaterally control the behavior of other humans. But this is only possible because we as humans possess 'bodies' which have the ability to control unilaterally the 'bodies' of other humans. Thus, since God has no body, such control is not within God's power. Or, stated differently, it might be argued that we as humans are able to be controlled unilaterally only by the use or threat of physical force and, thus, since God cannot use physical force, it still holds that God can only persuade.

But why should we grant that humans can only be unilaterally controlled by the use of physical force? Let us assume, for example, that someone discovers that a woman is having an extramarital affair and threatens to tell the unsuspecting spouse if not paid $10,000. And let us further assume that the consequences of discovery are so undesirable for our adulteress that she sees no option but to pay the blackmailer. It appears in this case that our adulteress has in a very real sense been forced to act against her will. But the force in question was psychological, not physical.

Or let us consider a more 'positive' form of psychological manipulation. Let us assume that a parent knows that his child wants desperately to be a sports hero. And let us further assume that the parent convinces the child that she cannot fulfill this dream unless she receives enough rest and that the child, therefore, willingly goes to bed whenever the parent says she should. In this case the child has not been forced to act against her will, but the control is no less real. The parent has, by the use of standard manipulative techniques, brought it about that the child desires to act in accordance with his wishes.

It might be argued that the 'control' in these cases is not really unilateral since our adulteress still retains the power to refuse to meet the blackmailer's demands and our child still retains the power to disobey the parent. In one sense this is true. Psychological manipulation, unlike physical manipulation, does not destroy the *capacity* of an individual to refuse to act in accordance with the wishes of the manipulator. But, given the value system of the adulteress, it is not clear that she would in fact even consider not paying the money. Nor, given our aspiring athlete's value system, is it clear that she would in fact even consider not going to bed. In short, it is not clear that individuals can in fact always resist psychological manipulation. Such manipulation does in some cases appear in a very real sense to result in unilateral behavioral control.

Nor can it be argued that successful unilateral psychological manipulation is not a widespread phenomenon. With proper training some of us might be able at times to recognize and resist even the most subtle manipulative techniques. But the well-documented ability of advertisers to manipulate our consumer activities and the media to manipulate our social and political perspectives bears witness to the fact that our attitudes and desires, and thus our behavior, can on the whole quite consistently and effectively be controlled apart from the use of physical force.

But what of the God of process theism? If we as humans can at times unilaterally control the behavior of other humans without the use of physical force, ought we assume that God could coerce in this sense? Could God, for example, make our adulteress experience enough guilt or fear of exposure to insure that she stops her illicit affair? Or could God, like the parent, also play upon the desires of the child to insure that she goes to bed? It seems to me that the answer to such questions is yes. Process theists, we have seen, believe that God has the ability to make each of us aware of the divine perspective at each moment. Thus, I see no reason to deny that the God of process theism has the power to bring it about that an adulterous woman becomes aware of the real possibility of exposure or that a child becomes aware of the fact that going to bed is consistent with her long-term goals. And process theists also believe, we have seen, that God has the power to bring it about that we feel some compulsion to act in accordance with the divine will. Thus, I see no reason to deny that the God of process theism could cause our adulteress or child to feel some compulsion to do the right thing.

But could the God of process theism insure that they would do so? It might be argued that such a being could not. God's capacity to lure, we might be told, is powerful enough to insure that certain motivating factors will be considered, but never powerful enough to insure that such factors will determine behavior.

Such reasoning, however, is not convincing. First, effective psychological manipulation is normally based on an adequate understanding of the character of the person or persons to be manipulated, not on some quantitative sense of manipulative power. For example, a person who is familiar with the thought processes and attitudinal dispositions of her spouse or child can frequently control or modify the behavior of either with a simple glance or short utterance. There is, accordingly, little reason to believe that a being who understands us totally and has the power to make us feel some compulsion to act in accordance with its wishes could not, by the judicious use of such power, manipulate our behavior upon occasions.

Second, according to process thought, God even has the ability to influence to some extent those individuals who are consciously choosing to live lives which are not in keeping with the divine will or who tend not to be influenced easily by others. But if this is so, is it not reasonable to believe that God at least has the *ability* to 'overwhelm' those who consciously choose to live lives compatible with God's basic aims or who are very easily influenced by others?

Lewis Ford, however, is not convinced. In response to an earlier appearance of this line of reasoning, he has written the following:

> Basinger speculates about the powers of psychological manipulation as a form of coercion, and wonders whether the process God could coerce in this sense.... Basic to [his] argument is the assumption that we are aware of God's initial aim. This, however, is rarely the case. For one thing, God's aims are seen as persuasively influential on all levels of actuality, most of whom, while enjoying subjectivity, have no consciousness at all. For another, consciousness emerges for complex actualities only in the later phases of experience (concre-

> scence), whereas the aim is operative from the first. There is plenty of opportunity for the aim to be completely distorted by the time it reaches consciousness.... It is this very indirectness of the consciousness of divine aim that insures its persuasive power. If we could unambiguously hear the divine commands, knowing that they were the very best for us, we should feel obligated to obey these commands without question.... But God cannot act in such a manner since the divine aims influence us directly only with respect to the subconscious.[16]

It seems to me, though, that Ford's comments are misguided. First, my general argument is not based on the assumption that we are consciously aware of God's leading. In fact, just the opposite is true. I am assuming that psychological manipulation is most effective when we are not consciously aware of the manipulating forces, since we are then unable consciously to react to them. This is true even when I specifically argue that God at least has the capacity to 'overwhelm' those who consciously choose to live lives compatible with God's basic aims. I am not, by this statement, claiming that we are consciously aware of God's leading. I am arguing only that those who consciously attempt to open themselves up to God's subconscious leading stand a better chance of having such leading become efficacious in their lives. And this concept is surely compatible with process thought. Griffin and Cobb, for instance, tell us that insofar as we genuinely open ourselves up to God's truth as found in the teaching of Jesus, "we are more open to the divine impulses in our experiences," and thus "more apt to respond positively to [them]."[17]

So I remain unrepentant. While there may well be good reasons why a being who has the capabilities of the God of process theism *would* never psychologically manipulate other entities, I see no reason to deny that such manipulation *could* be accomplished.

It appears, accordingly, that proponents of Griffin's argument face a dilemma. We as humans seem at times to possess the ability to control the behavior of other humans. If process theists argue that such control is not really coercive because those humans controlled retain some power of self-determination, their point becomes trivial. For the crucial question which the existence of evil requires all theists to answer is not whether God could take away all of our power of self-determination. The crucial question is whether God could, in a manner analogous to a parent controlling a child, control our behavior in some cases. If, on the other hand, process theists grant that humans can at times control other humans but argue that God cannot do so, then their position appears less than convincing or satisfying. For as we have seen, it appears that the God of process theism does possess the ability to control human behavior through psychological manipulation in at least some contexts.

Or to state the essence of this criticism somewhat differently, Griffin's argument appears to be fatally ambiguous. The question under discussion is whether the following claim is true:

(1) God will never unilaterally control the actions of other entities.

Griffin argues that (1) is true because a being can be controlled unilaterally only if it is devoid of all power of self-determination and not even God can bring about this state of affairs. But to say that God cannot cause a being to be devoid of all power of self-determination can be interpreted in two ways:

(1a) God cannot bring it about that other entities are totally devoid of the power to act independently in *any* sense—that is, are devoid not only of the power to act out their desires but even of the power to determine their own desires or in other ways control their thoughts.

(1b) God cannot bring it about that other entities are devoid of the power to act out their desires—that is, are devoid of the power to behave in accordance with their (possibly self-determined) wishes.

If Griffin is affirming (1a), then his argument is trivial because coercion is normally defined in terms of (1b) and, as we have seen, it does not necessarily follow from the fact that God cannot coerce in the manner described in (1a) that God cannot coerce in the manner described in (1b). And if Griffin is affirming (1b), then his argument seems unsound. For, as I have argued, it appears that the God of process theism could coerce in this sense.

But perhaps I have still been too hasty in concluding that (1b)—the claim that God could not unilaterally control behavior even if God desired to do so—is false. In *Process Theology: An Introductory Exposition*, Griffin (in collaboration with Cobb) argues that there are certain "necessary because uncreated principles governing the interrelations among worldly actualities."[18] One such necessary metaphysical principle (or set of principles) is based on what he calls, in another context, the "positive correlation between the capacity for intrinsic goodness, on the one hand, and freedom, or power of self-determination, on the other."[19] Experience is intrinsically good, we are told, "to the degree that it is both harmonious and intense." But increased intensity is said to require an "increased complexity which can bring together a greater variety of detail into contrast."[20] Griffin concludes, accordingly, that an "increase in the capacity for enjoying intrinsic goodness" necessarily means an "increase in the power to integrate harmoniously an ever-greater variety of data from the environment." And such power, he adds, "is one and the same thing as the power for self-determination."[21] In short, for Griffin it is a metaphysical truth that an actuality's capacity for enjoying intrinsic goodness rises in direct proportion to its power of self-determination.

But an actuality can only genuinely have the power to integrate the data in a harmonious fashion, he believes, if it also has the power to integrate such data in a disharmonious manner. Hence, he concludes that an actuality's capacity for experiencing or causing evil also necessarily rises in direct proportion to its power of self-determination.[22]

Grffin then goes on to apply these necessary principles to the relationship between humans and God, concluding that the freedom which is entailed by the capacity to enjoy human-level values is necessarily the freedom "to disregard the initial aim proffered by God in favor of some other real possibility for that moment of existence," a real possibility which may well, if actualized, generate significant disharmony.[23]

Moreover, Griffin argues, these eternally necessary principles are "not dependent upon a choice, even a divine choice." Rather, "any development which God can promote will have to conform to these correlations."[24] In other words, as Griffin sees it, God does not have the option of coercing us, even occasionally, because God is compelled by metaphysical principles which even Deity did not create, but to which it must conform, to use only persuasive power.

This is an interesting line of reasoning. But as support for the claim that to possess self-determination in relation to God is to possess the ability in every context to refrain from acting in accordance with God's initial aim, it is not convincing. If we assume with Griffin that the freedom which is entailed by the capacity to enjoy human-level values is necessarily the freedom "to disregard the initial aim proffered by God," then it may be that we can only be considered truly human in those contexts in which we have the power to reject God's wishes. But it does not follow from the assumption that there exists a necessary correlation between human-level values and self-determination that God could, in fact, never coerce us (unilaterally control our behavior). For example, it does not follow from the assumption that Hitler acted in a truly human fashion only in those instances in which he was not coerced by God that God could not have unilaterally controlled Hitler occasionally. To establish that God could never control our behavior, it must be shown that there exists some eternal, necessary metaphysical principle which allows only for the existence of actualities who are free to reject God's initial aim at all times. This Griffin has not done.

But there remains yet another way in which process theists might attempt to defend their contention that the God of process theism could never totally control our behavior. For the process theist, reality consists of a consecutive series of momentary actual occasions. Each such occasion is said to (a) "come into being as an experiencing subject," (b) integrate the data it receives from past occasions, God's initial aim and its own subjective reaction into a "unified experience" which it passes on to other occasions and then (c) perish as an experiencing subject.[25] But the integration mentioned in (b) can obviously occur in any meaningful sense only if God does not unilaterally control the actions of other entities. Accordingly, it might be argued, it can make no sense to ask whether the process God could coerce. It may be that another being with the capacities of the God of process theism could coerce. But to be a process theist is to affirm a view of reality which automatically rules out such coercive activity. Within the process system, the possibility of coercion is not an open question.

However, this argument simply fails to address the basic issue at hand. It is certainly true that if God were to exercise coercive power, the type of 'integration' central to the process view of reality would be destroyed. Thus, if we assume that the process conception of reality is accurate, it does indeed follow that God never *does* coerce. In other words, in this sense it is true that within the process system, the possibility of coercion is not an open question. But it does not follow from the fact that the God of process theism *can* (in the sense of *will*) *never* exercise coercive power that such a being does not possess the capacity to coerce. Or, stated differently, it does not follow from the fact that the use of coercion by God is not a debatable issue within the process system that the question of whether God has coercive capabilities does not remain open. For to grant that the God of process thought possesses the power to coerce in no way contradicts the claim that coercive power will never be exercised and thus that 'noncoercive integration' stands as a metaphysical given within the system. What process theists need to demonstrate is that something essential to the process system entails that God could never coerce, even if God so desired. But this, I continue to maintain, process theists have not done.[26]

Conclusion

The implications of my thesis for the process critique of classical theism are obvious. If I am correct—if it is true that a being with the attributes of the God of process theism could coerce other beings *in the sense in which we normally use the term*— then the standard process contention that its concept of God offers us a needed corrective to that found in classical thought—for example, more adequately accommodates meaningful senses of evil and freedom—is greatly weakened. For if the God of process theism can coerce but has simply chosen not to, then divine noncoercion ultimately becomes a moral choice as opposed to a metaphysical mandate. And if this is so, then process theism is, in the last analysis, practically indistinguishable from, and thus no more adequate than, those variants of classical theism in which it is also held that God has voluntarily chosen to refrain from significant (or any) unilateral involvement in earthly affairs.[27]

Chapter II

HUMAN COERCION

A FLY IN THE PROCESS OINTMENT?

'Coercion', we found in Chapter I, is a somewhat ambiguous term within process theology. In their standard metaphysical discussions, process theists[1] usually define coercive power as the power to bring it about that another entity is totally devoid of any degree of self-determination. But they uniformly agree that every entity always possesses some degree of self-determination (freedom). Thus, process theists uniformly deny that any entity, divine or human, can coerce in this sense.

But 'coercion', we saw, has a different, weaker meaning in normal human discourse. Take again, for example, the common contention that Hitler acted coercively when he placed Jews in concentration camps or the claim that parents are acting coercively when they finally pick up their recalcitrant children and make them go to bed or the common contention that a government is acting coercively when it refuses to give its citizens any opportunity to help formulate the laws by which they are governed. In such cases, the claim is not that Hitler or parents or government leaders have totally divested anyone of all power of self-determination. The claim is weaker: that they have unilaterally restricted the ability of others to act in accordance with their desires.

Process theists do not deny that coercion in this weaker sense occurs, at least on the human level. Charles Hartshorne, for example, speaks of the human "power of brute force" which at times results in the unilateral removal of political freedom or even in death.[2] W. Widick Schroeder observes that if coercion is defined as the capacity to act in ways violating the rights of others, then "persuasion and coercion interplay in any human community."[3] John Cobb tells us that if coercion is defined as the unilateral imposition of one's desires on another, then "no society can exist without some measure of coercion."[4] Even David Griffin acknowledges that since there are degrees of self-determination, "some activity can be called coercive in a relative sense."[5]

In short, process theists, like the rest of us, admit that at least on the human level we need to consider more than just two types of power: coercive power which would (if it existed and were applied) completely divest individuals of all of their power of self-determination, and persuasive power which never unilaterally forces individuals to act against their wishes. They acknowledge that there is an important form of nonpersuasive (weakly coercive) power which can unilaterally restrict or destroy the ability of individuals *to act* in accordance with their wishes.

In this chapter, I will discuss the normative status of this weaker form of coercion within process thought. More specifically, I want to discuss the following question: When, if ever, is it justifiable for a process theist to use, or condone the use of, coercion of this sort on the human level? Or, to phrase the question differently: When, if ever, can the process theist justifiably condone the unilateral restriction of someone's self-determination? When, if ever, can the process theist condone the use of nonpersuasive power?

I shall argue that in whatever manner the process theist attempts to respond, significant consistency problems within the process system develop.

Process Perspective on Human Coercion

Most process theists are serious metaphysicians with a strong desire to maintain an internally consistent world view. Thus, it should not be surprising that although process theists are very concerned with praxis—the practice of one's faith in the actual world—they strongly insist that all such activity must find its basis in one's doctrine of God. Cobb and Griffin at least implicitly criticize many of the liberation theologians for failing to do this.[6]

It seems best, accordingly, to begin our discussion of the

process position on the use of coercive power by humans by attempting to discern the attitude of the God of process theism toward it. As we discovered in Chapter I, most process theists believe that God cannot coerce in any sense. Divine power is for them always persuasive. God never unilaterally controls even the behavior of another entity. Moreover, they maintain that this purely persuasive posture is not the result of a moral choice on God's part. It is seen rather as the result of the outworking of certain metaphysical principles which necessitate that God exert only persuasive power.[7]

I argued in response that this line of reasoning is dubious, that given the powers most process theists grant to God, divine coercion in the weaker sense is possible. But I will grant for the sake of our present discussion that all divine power is necessarily persuasive. That is, I will grant that the God of process theism cannot in any sense unilaterally control any being's condition in such a manner that this being is restricted from acting in accordance with its will.

Unfortunately, this fact alone gives us very little insight into the moral status of human coercion. For there is, of course, no *necessary* connection between what we think is proper behavior —a moral belief—and what we can actually do—a descriptive fact. It cannot, for example, be justifiably inferred from the fact that I cannot personally feed all the starving people in the world that I would not approve of this being done by someone who had the requisite power. Likewise, it in no sense necessarily follows from the fact that God *cannot* coerce in any sense that God thinks that coercive power ought never be used by those who can exert it. To gain moral guidance concerning the use of human coercion, we must gain some understanding of the *moral* attitude of the God of process theism toward such coercion. We can best begin to do this, I believe, by considering the following question: Would the God of process theism occasionally coerce in the weaker sense if this were an option?

At times the process answer would appear to be no. God, all process theists believe, is perfect in every way. But divine coercion, Ford tells us, "whether limited or unlimited, is incompatible with divine perfection." Only divine persuasion possesses "inherent reasonableness... and is [consistent] with our best ethical and religious insights."[8] Griffin and Cobb seem to agree. Persuasive power, they maintain, "with its infinite persistence is in fact the greatest of all powers" since "the [persuasive] power to open the future and give us freedom is a greater power than the supposed power of absolute control."[9] Cobb is even more explicit in other contexts. "The only power capable of worthwhile results," he argues, "is the power of persuasion."[10] A similar theme is echoed by Hartshorne: "The ultimate power is the [persuasive] power of sensitivity, the power of ideal passivity and relativity, exquisitely proportioned in its responsiveness to other beings as causes."[11]

In other words, many process theists seem clearly to be saying that persuasive power is superior to (more perfect than) any form of coercive power. Thus, since they believe that God is ultimate perfection, it might seem that they would uniformly deny that the God of process theism would use any form of coercion, even if such coercion were possible.

But the issue is not this simple. A growing number of classical theists[12] (often labeled 'free will theists') believe that although God can coerce in the weaker sense, God has chosen as a general rule not to do so because a world in which there exists significant freedom and the potential for significant evil is superior to a world containing neither. That is, a number of classical theists believe divine noncoercion to be the result of a self-limitation on God's part. Now, of course, since process theists believe that God cannot coerce, we must expect them to disagree with the metaphysics of this classical position. But should process theists not agree with the moral stance inherent in the classical free will theist's position? If process theists believe that God would not coerce in any sense even if this were possible, should they not then be in moral agreement with those classical theists who claim that God has chosen not to act in a more coercive fashion even though such coercion is possible?

One would think so. But this is clearly not the case. In discussing the classical free will theist's position, Griffin, for example, asks why a God who can occasionally coerce does not more frequently do so "in order to prevent particularly horrendous evils?" The fact that this would violate our freedom, he contends, is not a sufficient reason, for "as precious as freedom is, is it so valuable that God should not override it every once in awhile, to prevent some unbearable suffering? After all, it would have taken only a split-second's violation of the world's freedom to convert Hitler, or induce a heart-attack on him. Surely, if God could reassert divine omnipotence from time to time, these kinds of things should be done."[13] Ford agrees: If "God has the power to actualize the good unambiguously, then his goodness requires that he do so, and that right early."[14] Cobb makes an equally strong claim.[15] In fact, it seems fair to say that the most common criticism process theists level against the God of classical free will theism is the claim that if such a being really existed and were wholly good, we should expect to see displays of divine coercive power more often. But if process theists really do believe that more coercion would not only be preferable but required at the divine level if it were possible, then it appears that they should also acknowledge that the God of process theism would coerce if this were an option.

What we find, then, in the last analysis, is that there is no obvious process response to the question at hand. When discussing the persuasive power of the God of process theism, many process theists explicitly argue that such power is morally superior to, and more effective than, coercive power and, thus, at least implicitly argue that the God of process theism would not use coercive power even if it were available. But when criticizing the concept of God affirmed by classical free will theism, most process theists *seem* to reverse their position by arguing that a being who can coerce should do so more frequently.

Or to state this seeming dilemma more explicitly, to the extent to which process theists support their criticism of classical free will theism by arguing that a divine being who can at times coerce should do so more frequently, the moral and utilitarian status of persuasive power is diminished. But to the extent to which they support the moral and utilitarian superiority of persuasive power by claiming that the God of process theism would not coerce even if this were possible, their criticism of classical free will theism is damaged. Process theists cannot have it both ways.

Critique of the Process Perspective

Which way, then, do process theists want it? I am not sure. Hence, we will consider the implications of both possibilities. Let us first assume that a perfect being would use only persuasive power and, thus, that since the God of process theism is perfect, coercive power would never be used even if it were available. If this is what process theists believe, then we might well expect them to criticize any use of coercive power on the human level. For if persuasive power is the greatest power in the world and is "the only power capable of worthwhile results," anything more than 'pacifistic persuasion' would appear to be unjustifiable in all cases.

At times, process theists appear to be sympathetic to this line of reasoning. They explicitly criticize much of the use of coercive force in our world. Cobb at one point even goes so far as to say that "if we would be perfect as God is perfect, then we will undertake vigorously to affect the course of events creatively, and that means by persuasion."[16] But, in the last analysis, most major process figures do not condemn the use of all coercive power—even all violent coercive power—on the human level. Hartshorne, for example, argues that we should always use persuasion when possible. But "it is quite another matter to exclude the use of force even where no superior method can be found. And there are such occasions. . . . There is a power of brute force which is going to be wielded by someone, and it had better be retained by the conscientious and intelligent as a last resort against the unscrupulous who would, if not thus restrained, gladly accept it as their monopoly."[17]

Cobb is equally clear in his opposition to much of the use of coercion we find on the human level. "Nevertheless," he tells us, "it is very clear that entrenched interests are normally extremely resistant to persuasion. They maintain their power by institutionalized and counter-insurgent violence which causes enormous suffering and numerous deaths. Against this, revolutionary coercion, including violent coercion, is sometimes justified." In fact, he goes on to argue, "a Whiteheadian cannot be an absolutist in opposition to violence. Just as there are possible justifications for inequality (and for the use of violence in its defense), so there are also possible justifications for resort to violence against existing structures of power."[18] Cobb even gives us one concrete example, claiming that "in Nicaragua the Christian conscience sided with the use of relatively limited violence to bring an end to massive structural violence by a corrupt dictatorship" and that "this is surely a gain worth the price paid."[19] Finally, Schroeder tells us that "in some instances, humans must use force to protect human persons and human societies from predators, both human and sub-human. Universal pacifism is not possible in the present cosmic epoch."[20]

However, is this stance consistent with the contention that God would never coerce even if this were an option? Such process theists are not just claiming that coercion does *in fact* produce good consequences. They are clearly making a normative claim: that such coercion is *morally superior, justified* and even *demanded* of the Christian in some contexts. But how can it be justifiable for us as humans to coerce willfully if God would never coerce at all? Or, to be more specific, if God would never use coercive power because persuasive power is morally superior and produces more worthwhile results, how can process theists justify the human use of coercive power in some cases? How can it become morally superior and more worthwhile for us?

I can conceive of two possible process responses. Some might argue that God and humans have somewhat different agendas with respect to human activity. Cobb tells us at one point, for example, that God's ultimate creative goal is to introduce "the possibility of a creative synthesis of the new with the old."[21] From this statement it might be inferred that God prizes the preservation of freedom more highly than justice. God is grieved by the unjust, oppressive uses of freedom by some humans. But God's primary goal is for each of us to be as fully self-creative as possible, even if such creativity results in human oppression, and this is why God would not unilaterally keep self-creative individuals from abusing the freedom of others even if this could be done. But the divine agenda for humans, it might be argued, is slightly more utilitarian. While God prizes freedom over justice, God wants us to prize justice over freedom. That is, while God will tolerate injustice for the sake of maximizing each person's creative option, God desires us to maximize the quality of freedom for the greatest number, even if this means we must at times unilaterally minimize the freedom of a few. And this, it might be concluded, is why we are encouraged to coerce occasionally even though God would never do so.

This line of reasoning, however, generates serious difficulties.

First, if freedom is from God's perspective a higher good than justice, then it is difficult to see why it should not also be so for us. Or, stated differently, if God so prizes human autonomy that a Hitler would not be coerced even if this were possible, then it is hard to understand why God would want us to do so. It would seem, rather, that we, mirroring the divine ranking of values, should also refrain from all coercive uses of power. Moreover, it is not at all clear that most process theists really accept this two-agenda model. Cobb, for instance, tells us that "process theologians are led, no less than others, to the view that the special concern of the Christian, as of God, is with the liberation of the oppressed."[22] Griffin agrees. God not only wills the end of oppression, he informs us, but is continuously active in the world toward this end. Thus, when "we, inspired by God, work toward such a society," we do so "not only for the sake of ourselves and our descendants, but also for the sake of God."[23]

Such statements are admittedly somewhat ambiguous. But they can easily be interpreted as saying that God and humans do share a similar agenda. That is, they can easily be interpreted as supporting the contention that God also believes justice (maximized freedom for the greatest number) to be more important in some contexts than the maximal preservation of freedom for each individual.

But if this is so, how can process theists still maintain that God would not use coercive power even if it were available? If God, no less than humans, wants to end oppression, and God desires us as humans to use coercion at times to accomplish this end, must not process theists grant that God would coerce if this were possible?

Perhaps not. God and humans, it might be argued, do share the same agenda with respect to the oppressed. But it is only for God that persuasion always has more worthwhile results than coercion.[24] For only God has immediate, constant access to every human, and only God knows the true motives behind each human behavior and how such motives can best be affected. Thus, only God can insure that persuasion will be maximally effective, and only constant maximal persuasion is always more effective than coercion. Where such persuasion is not possible, coercion is sometimes more effective than persuasion alone. This is why God sometimes approves of (lures us toward) coercion on the human level even though such coercive power would never be used by God even if it were available.

But this line of reasoning is also quite problematic. It may well be true that God can persuade more effectively than humans. But this fact alone tells us little about whether God would, or we should, coerce. If we assume, as we presently do, that the primary goal of both God and concerned humans is to maximize freedom (creativity) for the greatest number, it is the following question with which we must be concerned: Does divine and human persuasion, when combined with occasional human coercion, better maximize freedom than does continuous divine and human persuasion alone? If the answer is no—that is, if persuasion alone is as effective as or more effective than the combination of such persuasion and some human coercion—we have a sound basis for assuming God would never coerce. But why then would God approve of any human coercion? Since human coercion has absolutely no intrinsic value within a process system (in fact, is an intrinsic evil), it would appear that if persuasion is more effective alone, process theists should be pacifists. On the other hand, if the answer is yes—that is, if divine and human persuasion alone does not maximize human freedom to the extent that such persuasion and divinely approved human coercion do—we have a sound basis for human coercion. But why then would the God of process theism not use coercive power if this were an option? To grant that God would do so would not mean that God could no longer continue to apply maximal persuasion. Nor would it mean that such persuasive power was less effective than coercion. It would simply be to grant that God would use *all* the means available for maximizing freedom for the greatest number.

It seems to me that we must conclude, accordingly, that whether or not we assume that the God of process theism has the same agenda (goals) as humans, there is no good reason for assuming both that God approves of human coercion in some cases and that God would not coerce in this manner even if this were possible. One of these beliefs, it seems, must be dropped or modified.

But this may not be a serious problem for all process theists. We never meant to be read as saying that the God of process theism would never use coercive power if it were available, some might argue. We do believe God *cannot* coerce. But we have always believed that God would on occasion exert coercive force if this were possible.

To make this move has some obvious benefits. For example, it allows process theists to continue to challenge the moral integrity of the God of classical free will theism. Moreover, it certainly does create a strong theological justification for the type of coercion many process theists believe is necessary on the human level.

But again problems develop. For instance, once process theists acknowledge that God would at times act coercively if this were possible, they must radically revise some of their claims about the nature of persuasive power. They can still maintain that persuasive power is more consistent with freedom than coercive power and that persuasive power, when effective, has the most worthwhile results. And they can still claim that we should attempt to persuade whenever possible. But if the God of process theism would coerce if this were an option, then process theists can no longer maintain with Ford that divine coercion, "whether limited or unlimited, is incompatible with divine perfection." Moreover, process theists can no longer agree with a strong reading of Cobb and Griffin's claim that persuasive power, "with its infinite persistence is in fact the greatest of all powers." Persuasive power may be the ideal. But if God would coerce at times if such power were available, then it must be acknowledged that, in principle, the use of both persuasive and coercive power would at times be the best and most useful course of action. Nor can process theists continue to accept Cobb's claim that "the only power capable of worthwhile result is the power of persuasion." If God would use coercive power if it were available, then there are, in principle, times when divine persuasion plus divine coercion would bring about more worthwhile results.

But Ford objects. In responding to an earlier appearance of this line of reasoning, he states the following:

> I suspect what ultimately underlies [Basinger's challenge] is the assumption that God is a being in company with other beings. If we grant this, then God as the perfect being enjoys the highest possible kind of unity, which is simplicity. This, in turn, entails immutability. If from a process perspective we gainsay divine immutability then we must conceive God not as perfect being, but as perfect becoming.

> Determinate actualities act on others by efficient causation. Insofar as such causation restricts the freedom of present activities, there is coercion. If, as Whitehead argues, there are both the dimensions of being and becoming, with becoming as the more fundamental as that which brings beings into being, then the most perfect metaphysical exemplification must be of limitless becoming. The same conclusion follows negatively from Whitehead's observation that all determinate actuality, all beings, are necessarily finite. In order for God to be infinitely perfect, God cannot be a being, but only sheer becoming.
>
> Thus it is not true that God would be more perfect by possessing coercive as well as persuasive powers. Divine perfection requires that God be pure becoming, which lacks the possibility of coercion, which is open only to the efficient causation of beings. On the other hand, just because it is only appropriate for God to act persuasively need not mean that God cannot seek, on occasion, for creatures to act coercively. There are roles entrusted to finite actualities that an infinite actuality cannot fulfill. God's mode of operation is necessarily indirect.[25]

It seems to me that Ford's comments miss the essential point. It is certainly true that if God is *infinite becoming* and coercion is only possible for *finite beings*, then the God of process theism cannot coerce. And, of course, if infinite becoming exemplifies metaphysical perfection, then divine noncoercion is a necessary characteristic of metaphysical perfection.

We are not interested at present, however, in what God *can* do. We are interested in what God would do if certain powers were available. Thus the key question is whether God believes that the use of both persuasive and coercive power is in some cases most efficacious—that is, is most likely to bring about the best possible state of affairs. Ford seems to think so. Why else would he argue that God can justifiably "seek, on occasion, for creatures to act coercively?" But if a combination of persuasive and coercive power is in fact believed by God to be most efficacious in some situations, then divine coercion is not incompatible with *moral* perfection. It would be rather an exemplificaiton of it.

So I stand by my original contention. Once process theists grant that God would coerce if this were an option, they can no longer imply, as some do, that divine noncoercion has a moral basis—that is, they can no longer imply that a perfect being would for moral reasons never coerce. They must admit, rather, that divine noncoercion is an unfortunate metaphysical limitation, a limitation which God can attempt to overcome only by attempting to persuade us to coerce in those situations where this would accomplish the desired ends.

But to portray the God of process theism in this fashion will in the minds of many simply reinforce the most common classical complaint about process theism: that the God of process theism is a 'weak' being who is struggling to shape and control a world containing entities—for example, some humans—who in some respects have more power than God does. Process theists have most frequently attempted to counter this 'negative' divine characterization by arguing that, since God's primary aim is to maximize creative activity for *each* individual, God would never coerce even if possible. But this response is not available in the present context. The process theists we are now discussing grant that God would at times coerce if possible. Accordingly, it appears that the classical characterization in question is one with which such process theists must continue to grapple.[26]

Conclusion

It is important in closing that I clarify what has been argued. I have not argued that process theists cannot consistently allow for the justifiable use of coercion at the human level. My argument, rather, is that any attempt to demonstrate such consistency generates serious tensions within the process system. Ultimately, process theists must determine whether coercive force (in the sense in which they grant it is possible) would be used if it were available to God. If they decide it would not be used, they retain a strong basis for claiming that persuasion is morally (and possibly even practically) superior to coercion. But it is then very difficult to see why God would want us to use coercive power or how the classical God of free will theism can be criticized for not coercing more frequently.

On the other hand, if process theists decide that God would coerce if this were possible, they establish a sound basis for the human use of coercion in some cases. But they must then give up the claim that coercion is morally "incompatible with divine perfection" and the claim that persuasion is always the "greatest of all powers" and "the only power capable of worthwhile result." Furthermore, process theists must then acknowledge that humans possess a 'desirable' form of power God simply does not possess.

Moreover, whatever they decide, it seems fair to ask of them that they *clarify* their claims about the moral status of both persuasion and coercion on both the divine and human levels accordingly.[27]

Chapter III

EVIL

DOES PROCESS THEISM HAVE A BETTER EXPLANATION?

Here is a common situation: a house catches fire and a six-month-old baby is painfully burned to death. Could we possibly describe as "good" any person who had the power to save this child and yet refused to do so? God undoubtedly has this power and yet in many cases of this sort he has refused to help. Can we call God "good"?

B. C. Johnson[1]

Sometimes philosophers and theologians are said to be out of touch with the thoughts and feelings of average laypersons. But this is certainly not the case with respect to what is called the problem of evil. For over two thousand years, both 'professionals' and laypersons alike have struggled with the question posed above: If God exists, why is there so much seemingly unnecessary evil in this world? And ever since the question was first asked, theists have been attempting to respond. The purpose of this chapter is to assess the process[2] claim that its understanding of God's power vis-à-vis the world offers the basis for a much more adequate explanation (theodicy) than does any form of classical theism.[3] I shall argue that while process theism does offer us a plausible theodicy, it is not clear that its criticisms of classical theodicies are always coherent or that, even if coherent, such criticisms demonstrate the process theodicy to be superior to (more adequate than) that offered by some variants of classical thought.[4]

Process Perspective on Evil

We first need to identify more clearly the problem at hand. Why, exactly, is it that God's existence is thought by many to be incompatible with the evil we experience? The answer centers around three beliefs allegedly held by all theists: (1) God is perfect in power (omnipotent); (2) God is perfect in moral character; and (3) much unnecessary evil exists. A God who is perfect in power, it is argued, could prevent all evil, and a God who is perfectly good would prevent all unnecessary evil. But there is undeniably a great deal of unnecessary evil—for example, there is a great deal of unnecessary human pain and suffering. Hence, something must give. The theist must either forfeit her belief in divine omnipotence, divine guidance or both.

It is not difficult to anticipate how most process theists respond. They acknowledge that we do experience a great deal of unnecessary evil. And they adamantly contend that God is perfectly good in the sense that God is doing all that can be done to eradicate such evil. But they deny that to affirm God's omnipotence is to affirm that God could eradicate all evil. God is omnipotent in the sense that God has all the power that it is logically possible for a being to possess. But all actual entities always possess some degree of self-determination. Thus, it is impossible for any entity—including God—to control unilaterally any state of affairs. God, of course, deplores all the unnecessary evil we experience and is always attempting to persuade the rest of reality to help co-create the best possible situation. But since God alone can insure nothing, the fact that evil states of affairs eventuate (and sometimes even proliferate) does not count against either God's power or goodness.

Why exactly is this theodicy believed by process theists to be vastly superior to those affirmed by classical theists? The answer, as we have already implicitly seen, is based on the amount of power the God of classical theism allegedly possesses. As has been mentioned previously, not all classical theists believe that God always unilaterally controls all states of affairs. In fact some believe that God seldom does so. However, all classical theists do agree that God could unilaterally control all earthly affairs.

But if this is the case, most process theists argue, why does God not do more?[5] Why do we not see fewer children dying of painful diseases? Why do we not see fewer people locked in psychological torment? The only responses available to the classical theist, we are told, are that what we experience is not really unnecessary evil (we just mistakenly perceive it as such) or that God is willing to tolerate unnecessary evil. But the former is implausible and the latter impugns God's moral integrity. Only by positing a God who cannot unilaterally intervene can the problem of evil be truly solved. For only then can we both admit the reality of unnecessary evil and justifiably maintain that God is good.

Critique of the Process Perspective

Is this assessment accurate? Does process thought offer the theist the most plausible theodicy? I am not totally convinced. It must be granted that the process critique of classical theodicies is based on an intuitively appealing moral concept: A perfectly good being who *could* unilaterally control all earthly affairs *would* eradicate all unnecessary evil. But it is not clear that the process application of this principle to classical thought is always consistent or fair.

First, is it true, as process theists contend, that the God of classical theism could unilaterally remove all evil? In one sense it is. All classical theists do believe that God has the power to control unilaterally all earthly affairs, including all evil states of affairs. But the nature and extent of such power (control) differs radically within the classical camp. And this is something that some process theists do not always appear to recognize clearly (or at least acknowledge).

Let us take, for example, David Griffin's initial critique of classical theodicies in his book *God, Power and Evil: A Process Theodicy*. Classical theists, we are told, affirm "I" omnipotence, the belief "that an omnipotent being can unilaterally affect any state of affairs, if that state of affairs is intrinsically possible."[6] [Such power, it must be understood, is not simply the power to control what humans do. It is the power to control what humans freely do, since any actual human option is an intrinsically possible state of affairs. It is the power, for example, to control unilaterally what a Hitler *freely* does.] Thus, Griffin continues, classical theists must view all evil as only apparent (nongenuine). For if God can unilaterally control everything (including our free choices), then, of course, any evil which remains must be desired by God as a necessary component in the best of all possible worlds.

On the other hand, Griffin argues, process theists affirm "C" omnipotence, the belief that it is not logically possible for God to control unilaterally the activities of self-determining beings, even if such activities are intrinsically possible. [They deny, for example, that God could have unilaterally controlled Hitler.] Thus, Griffin concludes, process theists can admit that genuine (unnecessary) evil exists. And this makes the process theodicy more plausible than, and hence superior to, its classical competitors.[7]

Now, of course, it is true that some classical theists do affirm "I" omnipotence. They do believe God can unilaterally control everything, including what humans freely do. Hence, they must admit with Leibniz that all the evil we experience is desired by God. This does not mean that such theists must grant that all evil has intrinsic worth or that God enjoys it. But they must hold that just as a shot of novocaine—which has little intrinsic appeal—is 'welcomed' as a way of blocking the greater pain that would occur without it, or just as the hours of unenjoyable conditioning are a prerequisite to the joys of 'winning the game', the evils we experience are all necessary to produce the best possible world. Without even one instance of such evil, the world would on balance be of lesser value.

But the majority of philosophical theists in the classical mode do not view things in this way. They do maintain that God is in total control of all states of affairs in the sense that God initially created *ex nihilo* the world system out of which all states of affairs are generated and has the power to manipulate unilaterally any person or thing at any time. But they emphatically deny that this entails that God has "I" omnipotence—that is, that God can unilaterally bring about any logically possible state of affairs.

This point has been most effectively argued by classical theist Alvin Plantinga, whose general line of reasoning runs as follows. Consider two distinct possible worlds, W and W', which are identical in every way (except for God's beliefs about the future) until a time t, when in W a person named Bill freely chooses to steal an apple from a supermarket while in W' he freely chooses not to do so. And let us call this shared initial segment S. If Bill is in fact free with respect to stealing at this time, then while it is certainly the case that, given S, Bill might freely choose to steal the apple, or given S, Bill might freely choose not to do so, it is not the case that, given the actualization of S, Bill can both freely steal *and* freely refrain from stealing the apple at time t. That is, while it is the case that if S is actualized, Bill will be free to either steal or not steal, he can in fact make only one decision.

Now let us suppose that God, being omniscient, knows that, given S, Bill will freely choose to steal the apple. Then God cannot actualize W', that possible world in which Bill *freely* chooses not to take the apple. For to do so, God would obviously have to cause Bill to choose to do what he would not have freely chosen to do, given S—that is, God would have to make it the case that Bill was not in fact significantly free with respect to taking the apple in W'. On the other hand, let us assume that God knows that, given S, Bill will freely choose not to take the apple. Then God obviously cannot actualize W, that world in which Bill freely chooses to take the apple.

In other words, given that W and W' both contain S, it cannot be claimed that God can actualize just any possible world related to Bill. God's creative options are limited by what God knows Bill will freely do. God might, of course, decide not to create W or W' or decide not to make Bill free with respect to taking the apple and simply cause Bill to act in accordance with the divine will. But God cannot both make Bill free with respect to taking the apple and yet retain the power to create either W or W'. Thus, it follows that God cannot, as the proponent of "I" omnipotence maintains, actualize just any conceivable (possible) state of affairs.[8]

Or, to state Plantinga's point much more informally yet, God cannot unilaterally bring it about that we freely choose to perform good or evil activities. He can take away our freedom whenever this appears desirable and in this way unilaterally control us. But, if God has chosen to give us freedom, then God cannot unilaterally control the result. Much unnecessary, undeserved evil may in fact result.

Moreover, classical free will theists such as Plantinga believe that a world containing meaningful freedom and on balance more good than evil is a better world than one which contains neither. Thus, they hold that God is justified in allowing the unnecessary evil we experience even though God has the 'strength' to remove it. For to remove it would violate God's moral mandate to create the best *type* of world.

In short, classical free will theists affirm "C" omnipotence just as process theists do. Thus, they are immune from the standard process critique in question. They do not affirm the 'implausible' view that all evil is only apparent. They also maintain that much of the evil we encounter is gratuitous—the world would be a better place without it.

Most process theists, however, are aware of this 'free will' theodicy. Even Griffin, who initially talks as if all classical theists affirm "I" omnipotence, later acknowledges that some classical theodicists affirm "C" omnipotence. But he and John Cobb are ready with a response.

> There is a serious objection to this theodicy. It takes the form of doubt that freedom is really such an inherently great thing that it is worth running the risk of having creatures such as Hitler. If it were possible to have creatures who could enjoy all the same values which we as human beings enjoy, except that they would not really be free, should not God have brought into existence such creatures instead? In other worlds, if God could have created beings who were like us in every way, except that (a) they always did the best thing, and (b) they thought they were only doing this freely, should God not have created these beings instead?[9]

Process theology, they add, circumvents this problem because in process thought the relationship between freedom and value is necessary and not contingent.

> Traditional theism denied that there are any necessary because uncreated principles governing the interrelations among worldly actualities, and hence God's relations with them, other than strictly logical principles. This rejection of uncreated and hence necessary principles fits with the doctrine that the existence of finite actualities is strictly contingent, and that they were created out of absolute nothingness. If it is not necessary that there be finite actualities, and in fact they have not always existed, it makes no sense to talk about necessary principles governing their mutual relations and therefore limiting what God can do with them. But if there has always been a realm of finite actualities, and if the existence of such a realm (though not with any particular order) is as eternal and necessary as is

> the existence of God, then it also makes sense to think of eternally necessary principles descriptive of their possible relationships. . . . [T]his correlation between freedom and intrinsic value is a necessary one, rather than a result of divine arbitrariness.[10]

Such argumentation, however, is not convincing. First, the claim that "if it is not necessary that there be finite actualities . . . it makes no sense to talk about necessary principles governing their mutual relations and therefore limiting what God can do with them" is questionable in relation to the classical free will theist's position. Classical free will theists do believe that God has the power to create or not create finite, self-determining entities, but they strongly deny that the relationship between finite, self-determining entities and God's control over them is, therefore, not a necessary one. In fact, the contention that if God gives someone freedom, then God necessarily cannot unilaterally control its use is the basis for the free will defense. And there seems no reason to deny that the concept of such hypothetical necessity is intelligible.

Second, and more importantly, classical free will theists can challenge the claim that "if it were possible to have creatures who could enjoy all the same values which we human beings enjoy, except that they would not really be free, [God should have] brought into existence such creatures instead." The God of classical free theism certainly had the 'strength' to create pseudo-humans of the type Griffin and Cobb have in mind. But it is not clear that free will theists must acknowledge that God should have done so. For the creation of such pseudo-humans would have required God to deceive individuals in a significant and continuous manner with respect to the true nature of their self-determination. And it is not at all clear to free will theists that such divine deception is compatible with God's goodness.[11]

The process theologian might be tempted to respond by asking whether the creation of truly free individuals by the God of classical free will theism was worth the risk, given the potential for evil involved. But, as Griffin and Cobb acknowledge, the same basic question can be asked of the God of process theism: "Hence, the question as to whether God is indictable for the world's evil reduces to the question as to whether the positive values enjoyed by the higher forms of actualities are worth the risk of negative values, the sufferings."[12]

Griffin, however, is ready with another, related criticism of the free will defense.

> God could, on this hypothesis, occasionally violate human freedom for the sake of an overriding good, or to prevent a particular horrible evil. Of course, in those moments, the apparent human beings would not really be humans, if 'humans' are by definition free. But this would be a small price to pay if some of the world's worst evils could be averted.[13]

This criticism has an initial ring of plausibility, for it appears easy, from our human perspective, to identify contexts in which God could have profitably violated human freedom for the sake of humankind—for example, in relation to some of Hitler's actions.

But again, problems arise. First, as we have already implicitly seen in Chapter II, it is not clear that the standard process characterization of persuasive power is compatible with this line of reasoning. Most leading process theists appear to hold that the use of purely persuasive power is always morally superior to the use of coercive power because "the only power capable of any worthwhile result is the power of persuasion."[14] Thus, we might expect them to maintain that, since the God of process theism is a morally perfect being, this being would not coerce even if this were possible. But if even limited coercion is incompatible with divine perfection, then the current criticism of classical free will theism dissolves. For if the God of process theism can be praised because such a being would not use coercive power to eradicate evil even if this were possible, then the God of classical free will theism cannot be condemned for not using such power more frequently. In fact, such a being should also be praised.

On the other hand, if process theists really do believe that a morally perfect being would use coercive power to fight evil, then we must assume that persuasive power does not always produce the most worthwhile results and that the God of process theism, accordingly, would use coercive power to eradicate evil if this were an option. In short, we must assume that God's inability to fight evil with coercive power is an unfortunate metaphysical limitation.

Moreover, even if this tension can be overcome, the plausibility of Griffin's criticism may be deceiving. First, Griffin, himself, acknowledges that the free will theist can allow only the occasional violation of human freedom, and there is no way for us to know to what extent God has already profitably violated human freedom. Second, it may appear easy from our perspective to identify, in isolation, certain 'free choices' which we believe should have been vetoed by the God of free will theism. But what must actually be demonstrated to make Griffin's contention a strong one is that the entire world system (the different possible world) which contains such 'divine vetoes' would in fact contain a greater net amount of good than that found in the actual world. But it is difficult to see how this could be established in any objective sense.

Then, finally, Griffin's criticism has a questionable utilitarian ring. He suggests that the God of free will theism could profitably remove the freedom of a few for the good of many. But it is certainly not unreasonable for the free will theist to maintain that God so respects the self-determination of each particular individual that God will seldom, if ever, override those decisions which are significant in an individual's own life history, even if the actualization of such decisions will negatively affect large numbers of people.[15] Or, to generalize this point, free will theists can claim (plausibly, I believe) that God's respect for humanity severely limits the use of God's power to violate the freedom of individuals.

It appears, accordingly, that, as a criticism of the amount of moral evil we experience, Griffin's challenge has more psychological appeal than logical or evidential support.

But what of natural evil, process theists will respond. It is one thing to contend that God's respect for human freedom prohibits God from continually vetoing even those free choices which result in significant evil; it is something quite different to contend that such respect prohibits God from intervening more frequently in the natural environment. For it is surely reasonable to maintain that God could cure a small child of cancer or calm a very destructive storm without significantly affecting the integrity of human freedom or significantly lessening the amount of good which exists.

In other words, even if process theists can be convinced that classical free will theists have a somewhat plausible response to the problem of *moral* evil, most process theists will continue to deny that free will theism can offer a plausible response to the problem of *natural* evil. For only a God who cannot unilaterally intervene in the natural order, they will adamantly maintain, can furnish the basis for an adequate natural theodicy.

This is, admittedly, the process theist's strongest challenge. But as my brother, Randall Basinger, and I have argued previously, classical free will theism is not without a response.[16] The key to the process challenge in question is the assumption that there is little direct correlation between human freedom and the natural order. However, free will theists deny that this is the case. F. R. Tennant has argued, for example, that

> . . . it cannot be too strongly insisted that a world which is to be a moral order must be a physical order characterized by law or regularity. . . . The theist is only concerned to invoke the fact that the law-abidingness . . . is an essential condition of the world being a theatre of moral life. Without such regularity in physical phenomena there could be no probability to guide us: no prediction, no prudence, no accumulation of ordered experience, no pursuit of premeditated ends, no formation of habit, no possibility of character or of culture. Our intellectual faculties could not have developed. . . . And without rationality, morality is impossible.[17]

In other words, classical free will theists maintain that every possible world containing free moral agents must be a world characterized by regularity.

However, if this is so, they continue, it appears that God cannot unilaterally bring it about that all events in nature are perfectly correlated with the needs of specific humans—that is, it seems that God cannot unilaterally remove all natural evil. For it seems that to achieve such a correlation would require a myriad of special interventions in nature, and this would conflict with the necessity for regularity. Or, to state this important point differently, free will theists believe that if God's intention was to create free, moral creatures, and morality requires regularity, then there is a definite sense in which God's ability to control nature—including those natural occurrences which generate unnecessary pain and suffering—is necessarily limited.

It might be argued, however, that although such reasoning alleviates the problem of natural evil up to a point, another dimension of the problem remains unexplained. It is one thing to appeal to nature's regularities to explain why God cannot control how nature will affect particular persons, but it is something quite different to explain why God created the kind of regular system we experience. We might admit the need for a uniform system of natural laws, but why must this system contain horrifying, seemingly gratuitous types of evils—for example, tornadoes, earthquakes, and carcinogens?

In response, many free will theists argue that the recognition of the law-abiding, determinate character of nature also explains why our natural order, even though created by a wholly good and powerful God, might not represent the ideal state of affairs.

If nature is a determinate, law-abiding system, they maintain, it follows that we cannot insure the benefits of this determinate order without also allowing for the unbeneficial by-products which might follow from this very order. For example,

> If water is to have the various properties in virtue of which it plays its beneficial part in the economy of the physical world and the life of mankind, it cannot at the same time lack its obnoxious capacity to drown us. The specific gravity of water is as much a necessary outcome of its ultimate constitution as its freezing-point, or its thirst-quenching and cleansing functions.[18]

In short, beneficial aspects of the very determinate natural order that makes human life possible also necessarily make possible aspects not beneficial to human life. For the good and bad both flow from the same natural order. Consequently, to do away with all natural evils would entail doing away with the very aspects that make life as we know it possible. But if the very natural order that makes life possible logically implies the possibility of evil, God cannot be blamed for its presence.

Or, to state this line of reasoning somewhat differently, many free will theists argue that there is a meaningful sense in which God does not directly will natural evils. Such evils exist as unwanted, though unavoidable, elements of an otherwise good natural order. They are, therefore, genuinely evil both from the human and divine perspective. The only reason God does not prevent them is because preventing them would entail preventing the very determinate natural order that makes life possible.

> We cannot have the advantages of a determinate order of things without its logically or its causally necessary disadvantages.... The disadvantages, viz. particular ills, need not be regarded, however, as directly willed by God as ends in themselves.... They are not desired, as such, in themselves, but are only willed because the moral order, which is willed absolutely or antecedently by God, cannot be had without them.[19]

Process theists, however, may well believe more is needed. It is one thing, they might argue, to grant that a moral world must contain natural regularities and that some natural evil is an unavoidable consequent of such regularities, but quite another thing to grant that we must have the exact types and amount of natural evil which we in fact experience in the actual world. It seems possible to conceive of a natural order which, like ours, would make moral and rational life possible, but, unlike ours, would not contain features so alien and frustrating to the purposes of the very moral activity it supposedly makes possible. Moreover, if *we* can conceive of a natural order that would make moral activity possible without generating an excess of evil features, why did not the God of free will theism create such a world?

In short, it may well appear to many process theists that the God of free will theism could have increased the net amount of good in the actual world without damaging the integrity of human freedom simply by actualizing another world containing a less hostile natural order.

But the *prima facie* plausibilty of this contention, free will theists argue, is also deceiving. It is certainly possible to identify aspects of the present natural order which it seems could be profitably removed. It might appear, for example, that a world in which no tornadoes occurred or no cancerous cells developed would be superior to ours. But this is by no means a settled question. We are not simply dealing with isolated features within nature but with a whole determinate system. To make adjustments at one point will have effects elsewhere. Consequently, to dismiss specific unwanted aspects of our present natural order will not do. One must rather conceive of another entire determinate natural order which would neither imply the present evils, nor imply any similar or new evils, but still imply the goods that make human life possible. But this is certainly no easy task, at least for a finite mind. Moreover, with each advance in our scientific knowledge, the difficulty of this task becomes more apparent. "The more we know about the structure and interconnectedness of the physical universe, the less easily can we imagine alternative universes which retain the good features, but lack the bad."[20]

In other words, most free will theists contend that if those dissatisfied with their account of natural evil are not able to present a better world, free will theists do "not have to show that it was impossible for God to create a better set of world-constituents, or natural laws, or even that this is the best of all possible worlds."[21] The process critic, they acknowledge, can continue to hold that natural evil *might* not be justified in that there *might* be a better conceivable order. But unless some alternative system is presented, this remains only a possibility. And consequently, they conclude, free will theism can be said to offer an adequate natural theodicy.

It certainly seems to me that such a theodicy is adequate in the sense that it is internally consistent and, more importantly, does not deny either the reality of natural evil or the goodness of God. But is this theodicy adequate in the sense of being plausible? This is a more complex issue. Many process theists surely will continue to maintain that such a theodicy is highly implausible. And others may agree.

But I do not see why this should seriously bother the classical free will theist. Many individuals find aspects of the process system to be implausible. Yet, few process theists are overly concerned. They rightly maintain that as long as their system is comprehensive, self-consistent and most plausible to them, they are justified in affirming it. And the classical free will theist can, I believe, rightly respond in the same fashion. For, as Alvin Plantinga has forcefully argued, inductive inter-world-view discussions concerning metaphysical issues ultimately come down to a 'difference of opinion'—that is, the probability with respect to belief in such issues is ultimately relative to one's noetic structure.[22]

Conclusion

What, then, shall we conclude? Does process thought offer us the best theistic response to the problem of evil? I believe it does offer us a plausible theodicy. Given process assumptions about the nature of reality, it does follow both that much evil is genuine (unnecessary) and that God cannot in any direct sense be held responsible for it.

However, I am not convinced that such a theodicy is superior to that found in classical free will theism. Most process theists make this claim because they believe that a perfectly good being who could unilateraly intervene to remove unnecessary evil—for example, the God of classical theism—would do so to a greater degree. But, given their belief in the moral and utilitarian superiority of persuasive power, it is not clear that most process theists can *consistently* level this attack against classical thought.

Moreover, classical free will theists can offer a self-consistent account as to why a God who has chosen to create a universe containing significantly free individuals cannot unilaterally intervene to a greater extent. Such an account will not seem plausible to process theists. But since plausibility is a notoriously subjective concept, this negative reaction says more about the noetic makeup of process theists[23] than it does about the objective status of the free will theodicy.

Chapter IV

ESCHATOLOGY

WILL GOOD ULTIMATELY TRIUMPH IN THE PROCESS SYSTEM?

In the last chapter we saw that process theism[1] can offer a self-consistent response to the problem of evil. But many process theists do not believe this is enough. In the words of John Cobb and David Griffin, "Merely to see that the existence of a good God is compatible with evil does not suffice." Our concern must also be "that this evil be overcome or at least that we be assured that evil does not have the last word." In fact, they maintain that "a being who does not overcome this final threat of evil cannot be worshipped as God."[2]

Not surprisingly, process theists believe this challenge can be met. In fact most believe that, even though the God of process theism possesses 'less power' than the classical God, the process system offers a more religiously and philosophically adequate triumph over evil than that found in classical thought. The purpose of this chapter is to compare this process vision of hope with that found in classical theism.[3] I shall argue that, while coherent, the process vision is 'weaker' than is often acknowledged and that, even if this were not so, there is no objective basis for claiming that it is superior to the 'vision' found in classical thought.

Classical Eschatological Perspective

According to classical theists, our earthly realm is presently one in which good and evil commingle in a somewhat random fashion. For some individuals, peace and happiness are the primary experiences. Others experience primarily pain and suffering. But for most, some undulating combination of good and evil is the norm. Moreover, it is held that there is often little direct correlation between how one lives and what one experiences. The righteous often suffer unjustly while the unrighteous prosper. In other words, good does not always triumph.

But there is hope even in this realm, most classical theists argue. First, God's overall plan for our world cannot be thwarted. It is true that many specific occurrences are not (or at least appear not to be) in keeping with God's will. Disease, war and tyranny are realities. But God will never be defeated; God will never let things get out of hand. God still possesses the power to intervene unilaterally in earthly affairs and will use this power to preserve the world system in its intended form. We can be assured that God is 'still on the throne' and, thus, that God's purposes will be accomplished.

Second, they continue, God can and does bring good out of evil. Sometimes God does so directly. For instance, Christ was sent to transform the evil of 'the fall' into the triumph of 'the cross'. More often, however, God transforms evil into good through us. If we are willing to follow Christ's command to love our neighbors as ourselves, we can to some extent turn the tears of poverty, disease and death into joy. Things can be done. The good can in this sense triumph.

Finally, and most importantly, it is argued, this earthly commingling of good and evil is temporary. As things now stand, evil will never be totally defeated. However, things will not always stay as they are. At some point in time, either through a cataclysmic divine act or a gradual transformation, good will overwhelm evil and reign on earth. Evil may at times have triumphed in the earthly realm, but good will have the last word.

The earthly realm, though, does not exhaust reality for most classical theists. There is, they also maintain, a supernatural realm, which is itself divided into two distinct subrealms. One, usually labeled 'hell', contains only evil and the unrighteous. No joy or happiness is present. There is only permanent suffering. The other subrealm, usually labeled 'heaven', is where God dwells; it contains only goodness and righteous individuals.

Mental and physical anguish and all forms of sin are permanently absent. An eternal state of bliss exists. This does not mean that nothing happens, that no activity takes place. But nothing evil occurs. Even the possibility of evil is gone. Accordingly, in the supernatural realm we need not talk about the need for evil to be overcome. There is no undesirable commingling to worry about.

Furthermore, add many classical theists, this is the realm in which the 'scales are balanced'. We all have a strong affinity for just recompense. That is, we all feel that people should 'get what they deserve'. But while this obviously does not occur in the earthly realm, justice is meted out in the supernatural realm. The righteous spend eternity in 'heaven'; the evil spend eternity in 'hell'. Moreover, within these two subrealms, the exact nature of one's existence is tied to one's earthly actions. Everyone ultimately does indeed get exactly what he or she deserves. And this is the *ultimate* triumph of good over evil. Not only will the earth, itself, someday be purged of evil; all righteous individuals over whom evil triumphed on earth will exist in a realm where they, themselves, will triumph over evil.[4]

Process Critique of the Classical Perspective

Process theists agree with classical theists that we often experience evil "as an overwhelming destructive power against which we find ourselves quite helpless."[5] And process theists also agree that God attempts to overcome such evil by working with us to bring good out of it. That is, both classical and process theists hold that to the extent to which we cooperate with God, the real possibility of transforming evil into good is increased. Evil need not, in this sense, always triumph.[6]

However, apart from this single strand of shared hope, process theists must reject the outline for ultimate victory proposed by classical theists. First, process theists must, of course, reject the classical contention that God retains enough unilateral control over earthly affairs to insure not only that evil will never totally overwhelm good but that good will ultimately win out over evil. Evil might not totally overwhelm good. In fact good might begin to overwhelm evil. But from the process perspective there can be no guarantees. There is, for example, Cobb and Griffin tell us, "no assurance that the human species will move forward. It cannot stand still, but in the face of its massive dangers it may decay or even destroy itself."[7]

Lewis Ford, however, does not see this as an undesirable aspect of process thought. In fact, he tells us, not only is it not the case that a guaranteed triumph on the stage of earthly affairs is required by theism, such a 'guarantee' actually undermines genuine religious commitment. For if the final victory is indeed guaranteed, then there is no strive for it.... If its coming is inevitable, why must we work for it?"[8] On the other hand, he continues,

> The absence of any final guarantee now makes it genuinely possible for the expectation of the good to become a matter of faith.... The future is now doubtful, risky, uncertain. Yet the theist is sustained by his confident expectation that if we as creatures all have faith in God, that is, if all rely upon his guidance [given in the initial aim of each occasion], trusting him sufficiently to actualize the good which he proposes as novel possibility, then the good *will* triumph.... The world is a risky affair for God as well as for us. God has taken the risk upon himself in creating us with freedom through persuasion. He has faith in us, and it is up to us to respond in faith to him.[9]

Such reasoning, however, is in many respects not convincing. First, Ford's claim that any guarantee of a final victory will vitiate "the need to strive for it" is simply misguided in relation to most classical theists. Such theists do believe that good will at some point in the future triumph. But there is little basis for assuming that this assurance of a final victory should lessen the desire of classical theists to fight evil now. The coming of the final victory is inevitable. But such theists do care about those who *presently* suffer. And, as we have seen, they also believe some evil can in fact presently be overcome. Thus, they have every reason to "work for it" now.

Second, Ford's discussion of faith is problematic. If we define 'faith' as 'belief where there is less than conclusive evidence' (a cognitive definition) or 'commitment in the absence of objective certainty' (its affective counterpart), then it is certainly true that the process model for earthly triumph requires more faith than does the classical model. Within the classical system, the believer need not wonder whether (or hope that) good will ultimately triumph; victory is certain. Thus, the only type of faith required is faith in God—that is, faith that the classical conception of God is accurate. For if God really is the perfectly good unilateral creator of the world and has declared that ultimate victory is assured, then the issue is settled.

Process theists such as Ford must also accept by faith that their conception of God is accurate. But process theists have no guarantee that good will ultimately triumph, as do classical theists. So within the process system any conviction that good will ultimately triumph on earth must *also* be a matter of faith.[10]

But what does such faith really come to? It does not require an act of faith for the process theist to believe that God will continue to do all that can be done to bring about the triumph of good. Within the system this is a certainty. Moreover, even though process theists such as Ford often claim that persuasive power "is most effective in the long run," there is, by their own admission, no basis for even believing (having faith) that God can insure with a high degree of probability that good will ultimately triumph.[11] Thus, it appears that for process theists to have faith that good will triumph on the earthly stage can mean only that they have the positive conviction that we as co-creators with God will do what is necessary to bring about this desired end.

But how realistic is such faith? It is one thing to continue to believe strongly that things *can* improve and work toward this end. But it is something quite different to believe this *will* come about. The process theist certainly can hope things will improve. But I see no basis within the system for justifiably coming to believe (having faith) such improvement is probable. Furthermore, even if there were some basis for assuming that good will at some point triumph over evil on earth, there is no basis in process thought for assuming that such a 'triumph' would be 'ultimate'. Classical theists can make this claim because, within their system, God will unilaterally insure at some point that evil will never again triumph. But for process theism there is no end to the current system. All reality will continue eternally to be co-creative. Thus, even if good were to triumph at some point, evil might well reassert itself at a later time.

Moreover, the type of faith in question can hardly be called religious. It is only faith that the rest of creation will follow God's leading. Thus, there appears to be little basis for Ford's claim that the process eschatological perspective requires more 'faith in God' than does its classical counterpart.

Accordingly, I see no basis for granting that the process perspective on the ultimate relationship between good and evil on the worldly stage is superior to that held by classical theists. The two perspectives certainly differ. In fact, they are incompatible. But process theists have not demonstrated that their 'eschatological vision' for earthly affairs is more religiously or philosophically adequate than its classical counterpart.

Process theists must also reject the classical concept of victory over evil in the supernatural realm. The basis for such triumph, remember, is the classical belief that, while on the earthly stage good and evil commingle, no such interaction takes place in the supernatural realm. However, the process metaphysic expressly rules out such a distinction.

First, as was just implicitly mentioned, reality in the process system has been, is and always will be the outcome of a single, unchanging process. Each actual entity comes into existence, integrates its past and God's initial aim into its own subjective aim and then perishes. Such a process, of course, allows for radical change. While it started with God and undifferentiated unitary entities (chaos) and has developed into the complex universe we know today, it may at some point not only no longer contain humanity but not even contain any presently recognizable organic or inorganic form. However, there cannot be two distinct, isolated realms co-existing. All components of reality are, and always will be, integrated parts of a unified whole.[12]

Second, the eternal and necessary metaphysical principles said to control this process preclude the possibility of ever insuring the total and final separation of good and evil.[13] According to process thought, experience is good to the degree that it is both harmonious and intense. But, given that all reality is self-determining to some degree, it is impossible to insure that the experience of any actual entity will ever be totally harmonious and intense. It is always possible for any such entity to integrate the components of its experience in a disharmonious manner or forego productive intensity for triviality—that is, choose to create a less complex integration of data. And such disharmony or triviality is evil. Thus, the possibility of the commingling of good and evil must of necessity always exist.[14]

It does not follow from this, however, that process theists must deny the possibility of nonbodily existence, or even the possibility that we as humans will continue indefinitely or eternally to exist consciously after our bodily deaths. On such questions there can be, and is, a wide spectrum of opinion within the process camp. Charles Hartshorne, for instance, considers belief in immortality to be a "tall story" concocted by those who have not yet realized that "the world is not a kindergarten" in which all our wishes are granted.[15] Griffin, on the other hand, believes personal survival to be possible. In fact, while he cautions that this form of 'hope' cannot be a central tenet in process thought, he maintains that "insofar as much human life is characterized by more suffering than intrinsic good, the development of a post-bodily psychic existence could be one more example of God's overcoming evil with good.... (H)ope that our present human life, besides having its present intrinsic value, is also in part a preparation for a higher form of existence in the future, can add a final ground for affirming this present life."[16]

Cobb agrees, telling us that "belief in life after death, freed from its association with moralistic and punitive judgment, can go even farther than other forms of hope to sustain the affirmation of life and humanity." Even apart from such a hope, he adds, "we can declare human life good. But only with such a hope can we share in the affirmation that it is *very* good."[17]

However, it is hard to imagine exactly what this 'hope' can come to. For classical theists, the primary appeal of an afterlife lies in the fact that there will be a 'balancing of the scales' for all and the fact that the righteous will no longer encounter evil in any form. However, neither of these contentions can be affirmed by the process theist. As Cobb and Griffin both acknowledge, any form of afterlife would, from a process perspective, continue to be controlled by the same metaphysical principles which now control our existence.[18] Thus, since one such principle is that God cannot unilaterally bring about any state of affairs, we cannot, Griffin tells us, think of an afterlife as "providing an existence in which God would unilaterally rectify all the injustices in the present life."[19] Rather, as Cobb explains, the process theist "can think of God only as offering to each person in each moment of that other life whatever possibility of satisfaction he might attain, just as [God does] in this life."[20] But this means, of course, that God can no more assure the probability of a blessed, happy, just afterlife than God can assure the probability of such an earthly existence. In fact, given the process belief that any increase in the potential for good (harmonious intensity) also increases proportionately the potential for evil (disharmonious triviality), and the process belief in the radical openness of the future, it is possible that any given individual's afterlife would on balance be a much less happy, just state than was her earthly existence.

In short, the process conception of an afterlife leaves us with a very tentative hope. It does offer a chance for good to triumph over evil—that is, a chance for compensation for evil suffered in this life. But there can be no assurance. It is just as possible that evil would continue to triumph over good.

Process Eschatological Perspective

It is unfair, though, to assess the process 'vision of hope' solely on the basis of what has thus far been discussed. It is true that, unlike classical theists, process theists cannot assume that good will overwhelm evil on earth or in 'heaven' or that the 'scales will be balanced' for all in an afterlife. In fact it appears that process theists can assume even less along these lines than is sometimes claimed. But, by and large, process theists do not emphasize the forms of 'victory' central to classical theism. Rather, they emphasize a much different—less anthropocentric and individualistic—model of triumph.

As stated earlier, process theists believe that a being who does not overcome the final threat of evil cannot be worshippped as God. However, as Cobb and Griffin inform us, "this does not mean that God must prevent anything *we* regard as evil" for "much that we regard as evil is not geniunely so." For example, "we complain about our poverty or our failure to succeed in competition, whereas with spiritual maturity we can sometimes discover either that our poverty and failure have enriched our lives or that they have driven us to seek more important goods." To think otherwise is simply a reflection of our "immature desires."[21]

Moreover, they add, we must realize that much sin and suffering—for example, injustice or physical and mental anguish—"is necessarily entailed in the creation of beings capable of high grades of enjoyment." Thus, "rebelling against the universe because of this kind of evil reflects a misunderstanding not only of what perfect power can and cannot do, but also of the nature of evil, i.e., of the fact that triviality is as much to be avoided as discord."[22]

Nor, they continue, is the final problem even death, "for even untimely death need not destroy the meaning and worth of the life that has been lived."[23]

But if the ultimate evil is not really injustice, physical suffering, mental anguish or even death, then what is it? It is, in the words of Whitehead, "the fact that the past fades, that time is a 'perpetual perishing'."[24] Or, as Cobb and Griffin put this point, the real problem is temporality. It is the seeming fact that, although there is much enjoyment and intrinsic value in our present experiences, "everything we accomplish and enjoy will pass into oblivion." For if the "perpetual perishing of everything we value is the whole story, then life is ultimately meaningless" and our zest for living rightly disappears.[25]

However, process theists are quick to point out that God is clearly victorious over this evil. First, God not only experiences what each actual entity experiences. Such experiences are preserved everlastingly in the divine mind. Or, as Hartshorne puts this point, "what is indeed immortal . . . is precisely this finite series of experiences and deeds."[26] And, thus, in the words of Cobb, "neither individual death nor the extinction of the human race will be so total a loss as it otherwise appears. Even our little virtues and petty triumphs are not ultimately in vain."[27]

Furthermore, God not only retains the past, God also transforms or transmutes it into a harmonious whole. When God first encounters the past—the accumulated set of experiences of the world—it contains much that is intrinsically evil. There is much mental and physical anguish and much natural disharmony. However, as Ford tells us, God "can bring harmony to discord by interrelating potentially disruptive elements in constructive ways

... thereby achieving a maximum harmonious intensity from any situation."[28] Or, stated differently, all disharmonious aspects of reality are ultimately reconciled in the mind of God and in this way are not only redeemed but have meaning, value and purpose conferred on them as specific events.

It has been argued, though, that while this latter form of redemption is fine for God, it is not a significant form of a triumph for us.[29] It may be that God overcomes all evil by blending it with the rest of reality into what is experienced as a harmonious whole. But we are still left to experience disharmony—that is, evil is not overcome for us. Griffin, however, has a ready response. Evil, he tells us, is not only overcome in the divine mind. It is also overcome in the sense that God, "in responding to the evil facts in the world, provides ideal aims for the next stages of the world designed to overcome the evil in the world." In fact, he tells us, "this 'overcoming' in God is precisely for the sake of overcoming evil in the world."[30]

Such a response, however, is only partially satisfying. Griffin does, I believe, dispel the picture of a God who is interested only in a harmonious divine state of mind. But a crucial sense of asymmetry remains. In God harmony is always achieved. Evil is in this sense *always* overcome. But the appropriation of this overcoming is only a *possibility* for us since finite entities remain free to accept or discard what God offers. In fact, given that our lives are inextricably tied to the lives of all other finite entities, we could only totally appropriate the ultimate harmony (ultimate overcoming) experienced by God if all reality were simultaneously to follow God's leading—an extremely unlikely happening. Hence, our own experiencing of the fruits of this form of victory can at best be occasional and partial.

There is, however, a stronger, more personal sense in which most process theists feel that the divine integration of all into a unified whole can offer us triumph over evil. As process theists rightly point out, classical theists usually have a highly anthropocentric eschatology. Humanity is believed to be the most significant aspect of creation. Thus, the ultimate earthly triumph is seen as the overcoming of what is evil to humans, and much of the spiritual realm is often though to exist primarily to reward and punish human activity.

However, process theists view humanity differently. As has already been mentioned implicitly, 'good' and 'evil' from a process perspective are ultimately interpreted in terms of two criteria: harmony and intensity. Acquiescene to harmony (beneficial adaptation)at the expense of a more complex variety of distinct experiences (intensity) is the basis for one type of evil: triviality. The demand for more variety of experience at the expense of harmony is the basis for the other type of evil: discord. What is needed to maximize the good in any context is a proper balance of the two. Hence, since God is perfect in every way, God's creative goals reflect this fact. God does not strive solely to increase intensity or eliminate discord. God's primary creative purpose has always been (and will always be) to bring about the "maximum attainment of intensity compatible with harmony that is possible under the circumstances of the actual situation."[31]

Accordingly, while it may be true that humanity is, to date, the "supreme work of God on this earth," humanity cannot be viewed within process thought as the fulfillment of some ultimate creative purpose.[32] For, given God's true creative goals, "it is quite conceivable," in the words of Ford, "that in time [the evolutionary process] might bypass man and the entire class of mammals to favor some very different species capable of greater complexity than man can achieve."[33]

Nor can we even assume that God's primary creative goal at present is to insure the maximum amount of harmonious intensity for *humans*. For example, Cobb tells us, there is no evidence "that God would seek to persuade a malarial mosquito to starve rather than feed upon a human being."[34] God does, of course, have to adjudicate between the incompatible goals of various entities. But God does not always give preference to the higher order entities—that is, to those who have the capacity for a greater amount of harmonious intensity. Rather, Cobb continues, "God seems to call every living thing to a self-actualization in which immediate satisfaction looms large... even at the price of endangering harmony and order."[35]

In short, according to process theists, we cannot primarily assess 'cosmic success' in terms of human comfort. God does care about us. God does not want us to experience unnecesary mental and physical anguish; God does want us to work to eradicate such evil in the lives of others. But the ultimate good is harmonious intensity; the ultimate evil is disharmonious triviality. This is why process theists believe it can meaningfully and truthfully be said that good always triumphs over evil in God's mind. For God is always able to integrate the discordant aspects of reality into a harmonious whole with a more promising future. And this is why they believe that God has to date also been quite successful in bringing about the triumph of good (in this ultimate sense) in the world. As Ford tells us, God has been able to bring this mighty universe into being out of practically nothing.[36]

But how is all of this to give us a strong, personal sense of hope and meaning? How is this understanding of success to help us significantly experience the triumph of the good? It is here that we encounter the process concept of 'Peace'. As long as we continue to think primarily in terms of personal gratification (as classical theists do), the ultimate victory of good over evil will mean little to us. But to the extent we align ourselves with God's purposes—take God's goals as our own—we can personally experience Peace—that "Harmony of Harmonies" which excludes "restless egoism." For then we are opened up to experience that ultimate significance which comes with knowing we have made our particular contribution to 'the good'.[37] In other words, once we begin to see reality as God sees it, we will begin to experience the harmony (triumph) which God experiences. Or as Ford puts it, in this way we can "participate in the divine life through an intuitive foretaste of God's experience.... It is here that the good finally triumphs in all her glory—or, more precisely, as engulfed by all the divine glory as well."[38]

Critique of the Process Perspective

Much of this process 'vision of victory' seems to me to be perfectly coherent. It is, of course, not the same type of victory as that proposed by classical thought. And as such, it may not be appealing to some. But this fact in no way counts against the coherence of the process model. It simply indicates something about the 'eschatological taste' of such critics. I do, though, believe that the process model of triumph generates one substantive dilemma for process thinkers.

As we saw in the last chapter, process theists believe that their response to the problem of evil is vastly superior to that found in any form of classical thought. In fact, I believe it safe to say that most process theists consider this to be the point at which process theism is most superior to classical theism—even classical free will theism. The basis for this belief, remember, is the process contention that if God could coercively do more to eradicate the horrible evils we encounter (as classical theists believe), God should do so. Of course, as Griffin admitted, this might entail taking away our humanity, "if 'humans' are by definition free. But this would be a small price to pay if some of the world's worst evils could be averted."[39]

What are these horrible evils—some of the "world's worst"—which process theists have in mind? Their discussions make it clear that they are almost always talking in this context exclusively about the incalculable amount of injustice, physical suffering and mental anguish we experience. In other words, what the process claim to a vastly superior theodicy almost always comes down to is this: classical theism—even classical free will theism—can offer no morally justifiable reason for the existence of all the horrible physical and mental anguish we experience.

But we have seen that the emphasis changes radically when process theists turn to their model of ultimate triumph over evil. In this context, the ultimate evil "is not finally injustice, physical suffering or mental anguish."[40] In fact, Cobb and Griffin go so far as to say that "much of what we regard as evil"—for example, much of "our poverty or our failure to succeed"—is not geniunely so, and that to think otherwise often simply reflects the "immature desire" to avoid all discord, even at the expense of growth.[41] The ultimate evil, we find, is identified as temporality or 'perpetual perishing'—that is, the fact that the past fades—for "if everything we accomplish and enjoy will pass into oblivion . . . then life is ultimately meaningless."[42] But such is not actually the case, we are told. God not only preserves all experiences everlastingly. God continuously integrates such experiences—including the evil ones—into a harmonious whole which gives meaning, value and purpose to them all.

However, if *this* is the ultimate problem of (and solution to) evil, then is not classical theism as adequate as process thought?

Cannot classical theism resolve exactly the same problem in exactly the same way? Cobb and Griffin think not:

> Traditional theology has dealt with the evil involved in temporality by contrasting God's eternity with our temporality. But this is exactly the wrong solution. Whitehead wrote: "So long as the temporal world is conceived as a self-sufficient completion of the creative act, explicable by its derivation from an ultimate principle which is at once ultimately real and the unmoved mover, from this conclusion there is no escape: the best we can say of the turmoil is, 'For so he giveth his beloved—sleep'." Whitehead's point is that in such a vision we can contribute nothing to God, the converse of which is that God cannot save our experiences from final meaninglessness. The most that would be possible is endless ongoingness. But endless ongoingness would only protract forever the perpetual perishing that is the utlimate evil.[43]

Such reasoning may hold in relation to some strongly predestinarian variants of classical thought. But it does not hold in relation to classical free will theism. For free will theists, this world is not the self-sufficient completion of the creative act in the sense outlined by Whitehead. God did create *ex nihilo*. However, God is not the immutable, all-controlling God of Thomistic thought. God chose to create a world in which we possess meaningful freedom and, by doing so, voluntarily surrendered total control over much that occurs. Accordingly, much of God's influence must be indirect. To attempt to accomplish the divine goals, God must experience with us and then give guidance based on the actual state of affairs at any moment. But this is simply another way of saying that the God of free will theism, in a manner analogous to the God of process theism, not only preserves all experiences everlastingly but also integrates them into a harmonious whole which confers meaning on them and from which flows God's leading for our lives. In short, the same basic solution to the ultimate problem of evil proposed by process theism *is* also available to classical free will theism.

If this is so, however, then process theists are faced with an obvious dilemma. If the real problem of evil is the loss of ultimate value and meaning caused by perpetual perishing, then the theodicy affirmed by classical free will theists is quite adequate, and, accordingly, it is quite misleading for process theists to emphasize only the 'lesser evils' of physical and mental anguish when assessing it. On the other hand, if the real problem of evil is the physical and mental anguish we experience, then the process vision of hope disappears. For by its own admission, process thought offers no guarantee for victory over (in the sense of alleviation from) such evils in this world or another.

Or, to state this important point differently, the type of evil which must be considered ultimate in order to allow process theism to talk of an ultimate triumph over evil is different from the type of evil which must be considered ultimate if the basic process critique of the classical response to evil is to be at all effective. If perpetual perishing is the ultimate evil, then the process vision of hope stands, but only at the expense of the process critique of classical theodicies. If physical and mental anguish is the ultimate evil, then the process critique of classical theodicies retains whatever initial strength it had, but at the expense of the process model of triumph. There is an inverse relationship between the two. Something within the process system must be adjusted.

Conclusion

What, then, ought we conclude about the process perspective on the ultimate triumph of good over evil? Process theists do, I believe, offer us a self-consistent 'vision'. Moreover, the competing 'vision' offered by classical theism—even classical free will theism—is not without its own alleged difficulties. For example, as Lewis Ford has pointed out, if classical free will theists believe that God's respect for human freedom is so great that it causes God to allow much unnecessary evil on earth, then why should they expect God to insure a supernatural realm free from all evil? Wouldn't this undermine human *freedom* in this context?[44]

But even if we grant that such dilemmas are significant, process theists have still not established that their model of triumph is *superior* to that found in classical theism in the ways they usually claim—that is, that it allows for more faith or more powerfully motivates us to work for the good. Furthermore, the process vision[45] still undercuts the process critique of the classical response—especially the classical free will response—to the problem of evil in that it downplays the type of evil required to make the critique effective.

Chapter V

PETITIONARY PRAYER

DOES IT MAKE ANY SENSE IN A PROCESS SYSTEM?

All Christian traditions, including the process tradition, emphasize the importance of prayer. That is, all Christians are exhorted to communicate with (share with, talk to) God. Moreoever, within most traditions it is quite clearly held, to use the words of David Mason, that believers "are to ask God for things" and that God "hears, is affected by our importunities, and responds adequately to them."[1] In short, most Christians emphasize the significance of petitionary prayer.

But what of process theists?[2] They clearly affirm the importance of prayer. But do they believe we should engage in *petitionary* prayer? Some do. Moreover, they believe such prayer to be efficacious. That is, they believe such prayer 'changes things'. I shall argue, however, that there is no basis for retaining the concept of efficacious petitionary prayer within the process system.

Classical Perspective on Petitionary Prayer

The best way to begin this discussion, I believe, is to contrast the process perspective on petitionary prayer and its efficacy with those perspectives found in classical Christian thought. As we saw in the Introduction, proponents of classical thought believe that God initially created the world *ex nihilo*. Moreover, they believe that although God at that time established certain natural laws (psychological and physical) which are responsible for much of what we now experience, God has retained the power to intervene unilaterally in earthly affairs at any time. That is, God has retained the power to modify or circumvent the natural order.

Such classical theists[3] can be divided into two basic camps. One group affirms what I shall call specific sovereignty.[4] God, they believe, has total control over everything in the sense that all and only that which God wants to occur will occur. This world represents God's preordained, perfect plan. God could have created any number of self-consistent systems, but God chose to create exactly what we now have. Some in this camp claim that God retains such control by directly bringing about all states of affairs, including what we as humans 'freely' do. Others take a less deterministic approach. God does not control by directly determining everything. Rather, God foresees what will occur 'naturally' and then intervenes to prohibit or modify any action seen as incompatible with the divine will.

But in whatever manner the means of divine control are explicated, all proponents of specific sovereignty deny that God is in any sense dependent on human choice. God may use human choice as a means to accomplish desired goals. But our choices, and thus our activities, never thwart or hinder in any way God's perfect plan.

The implications of this model of sovereignty for petitionary prayer are obvious. If it can never be the case that any human activity can thwart God's plan, then of course petitionary prayer cannot be efficacious in the sense that unilateral divine activity is sometimes dependent on human requests. It cannot, for example, be the case that God at times gives wisdom to world leaders or watches over loved ones just because such wisdom or safety was requested. God may well become involved in such states of affairs, and God may even do so in the manner requested. But if such activity is part of God's eternal plan, it will occur regardless of whether God has been petitioned. Human assistance is not necessary.

Proponents of specific sovereignty have always strongly denied, however, that this means that petitionary prayer effects no real change and is thus pointless. Thomas Aquinas, for example, argued that

> . . . we pray not in order to change the divine disposition, but for the sake of acquiring by petitionary prayer what God has been disposed to be achieved by prayer.[5]

John Calvin maintained that

> . . . prayer is not so much for his sake as for ours. . . . It is very much for our interest to be constantly supplicating him: first, that our heart may be always inflamed with a serious and ardent desire of seeking, loving and serving him, while we accustom ourselves to have recourse to him as a sacred anchor in every necessity; secondly, that no desire, no longing whatever, of which we are ashamed to make him the witness, may enter our minds, while we learn to place all our wishes in his sight, and thus pour out our heart before him; and lastly, that we may be prepared to receive all his benefits with true gratitude and thanksgiving, while our prayers remind us that they proceed from his hand.[6]

Martin Luther agreed:

> God did not command prayer in order to deceive you and make a fool, a monkey of you; he wants you to pray and to be confident that you will be heard. You must present your need to God . . . in order that you may learn to know yourself, where you are lacking.[7]

In short, proponents of specific sovereignty argue that petitionary prayer is efficacious in the sense that it affects the petitioner and/or is a causal component used by God to bring about desired ends. For example, proponents of specific sovereignty believe that our prayers for guidance and safety are efficacious in the sense that they help us better see what we might do, help us remember that such wisdom and safety ultimately come from God, and/or stand as part of the preordained 'means' by which God has determined to bring about desired ends.

Unfortunately, process theists often tend to lump all classical theists into this specific sovereignty category and thus view the types of efficacy just outlined as the sole classical bases for petitionary prayer.[8] But, as we have already implicitly seen, a significant number of classical theists do not affirm specific sovereignty—that is, they *do* deny that God unilaterally insures that all and only that which God desires occurs.[9] They believe that a person can be significantly free with respect to an action only if God does not control what this person chooses to do. Thus, they conclude that to the extent to which God gives us significant freedom, control over earthly affairs is forfeited. If free, we may choose to do what God desires. But then again we may not.

Accordingly, those in this theological camp—which I shall here call proponents of general sovereignty—are not limited to explicating petitionary prayer in the same manner as that done by proponents of specific sovereignty. They do, of course, believe prayer to be efficacious in the sense that it affects the petitioner and/or is a component used by God to bring about desired ends. But many proponents of general sovereignty also believe that petitionary prayer can be efficacious in the exact sense denied by proponents of specific sovereignty. They do in fact believe that it is sometimes the case that unilateral divine activity is dependent on human petitioning.

Such efficacy is sometimes tied to human freedom. God, it is acknowledged, knows our needs even better than we do. Moreover, God loves and thus wants to help us. But God's primary creative priority was to create a context in which humans could function as free, responsible moral beings. And out of respect for such freedom, God must to a significant extent refrain from intervening in human affairs until requested to do so. Or, to state this line of reasoning somewhat differently, the argument is not that God does not want to do more than will in fact be done if no petition is offered. It is rather that the very concept of freedom on which God's initial creative act was based stands as a barrier to such uninvited intervention.[10]

This model, of course, is not intended to justify petitions offered for others. It is not intended, for example, to justify prayers in which God is asked to help resolve the marital problems of friends. For if God will not normally intervene until requested out of respect for the freedom of the petitioner, then surely God would not, at the request of a petitioner, intervene uninvited into someone else's life. However, this 'freedom model' does in the mind of its proponents constitute a plausible basis for affirming the type of efficacy in question for prayers in which the petitioner freely requests guidance or comfort for herself.

Other proponents of general sovereignty offer a broader, relational justification for this type of efficacy. God, they argue, deeply desires a meaningful relationship with us. However, a meaningful relationship of this sort can be developed and maintained only if God does not dominate or spoil us. Thus, in order to encourage us to stay in communication, God does at times refrain from giving us or others what God desires to give until it is requested.[11]

Process Perspective on Petitionary Prayer

Process theism, of course, cannot affirm any of these classical models of petitionary prayer. All are based on the assumption that God can, and at times does, *unilaterally* bring about certain states of affairs. But, within process thought, as we have already seen, this type of divine activity is impossible. The God of process theism is certainly active in the world. God is affected by every action, every desire, every event. And at every moment God shows loving concern for every creature by considering its past, "envisioning its best possibilities in its given circumstances, and by offering to every creature the ideal aim for it to actualize in each new present context."[12] Or, stated differently, at every moment, God presents to every creature the optimum real possibilities open to it. But all entities (human or subhuman) always have some power of self-determination. That is, in every situation, each entity to some degree fashions its own subjective self-determining response to its past—that which has happened in the world in which it finds itself—and God's presentation of the best future possibilities. Thus, in neither the moral nor natural realm can God unilaterally insure that certain things will occur.[13]

What then is left for process theism to say about prayer? Must it be considered superfluous? Many process theists clearly want to deny this. That is, they want to deny, to use the words of Norman Pittenger, that petitionary prayer "is absurd and irrelevant."[14] But if petitionary prayer cannot be efficacious in the sense that it initiates unilateral divine activity or even in the sense that it convinces God to become more involved than would otherwise be the case, is there still a sense in which such prayer can be seen as meaningful and significant?

In a recent essay, process theologian Marjorie Suchocki has emphatically declared that for at least one common type of petitionary prayer—intercessory prayer for others—the answer is yes. First, she argues, intercessory petitions are efficacious in the life of the person offering the prayer. When we pray, "we are changing the reality of our past" in the sense that we have raised to the conscious level new thoughts about the object of our petitions. And since, according to process thought, our decisions are always conditioned by our past, this new consciousness will necessarily have some effect on our present and future behavior.[15]

Let me try to illustrate what I think Suchocki has in mind. Assume that I pray for an ailing aunt. Such a prayer will raise to the conscious level thoughts about my aunt which, on this model, become a permanent component in my set of life experiences. And since I always make my decisions in the context of my life experiences, such thoughts will in some sense necessarily affect my future behavior toward my aunt. The effect may in part be direct and immediate. For instance, praying for my aunt may trigger a desire to call or visit or send a note. Or the effect may in part be delayed. Perhaps conscious thoughts generated during my time of prayer will resurface months later and trigger some beneficial activity. Moreover, my response may not always be as it should. I may, for instance, decide not to visit because it would be inconvenient or because I do not know what I would say. But the conscious thoughts generated by my prayer for my aunt will, given Suchocki's analysis, affect my life. They will make a real difference.

I see no reason to deny that intercessory petitions are efficacious for the process theist in this sense. However, some important qualifying remarks are necessary. First, this type of efficacy is not limited solely to the process model. All classical theists, as we have seen, grant that petitionary prayer affects the petitioner. And it is certainly compatible with classical theism to claim that intercessory petitions affect the person offering the prayer in the way just outlined.

Second, there is an important sense in which the concept of

prayer, especially the concept of *intercessory* prayer, is somewhat irrelevant to the type of efficacy under discussion. An instance of intercessory praying in this context is not efficacious because the request for intercession has itself elicited some response or even because it is a prayer. What produces the efficacy is the fact that certain conscious thoughts come into the mind of the petitioner during prayer. And although praying to God about someone or something is certainly one way in which such conscious thoughts might be generated, it is certainly not the only, or perhaps even the best, way in which this can be accomplished. Perhaps, for example, generating conscious thoughts about certain persons or things by talking with friends would be more efficacious in the sense in question.

In short, it seems that the type of efficacy under discussion is best seen as a potentially beneficial by-product of intercessory petitioning. Thus, it is debatable whether either the process (or classical) theist can legitimately appeal to such efficacy as a primary reason for such prayer.

Suchocki, however, believes that there are other ways in which intercessory prayer affects the petitioner. According to process thought, she reminds us, God is at each moment attempting to persuade us to actualize the optimum real possibilities open to us. And when we pray, we change "the reality with which God works," and "the reality of the world has a real effect upon which possibilities may efficaciously be given."[16] In other words, when we through prayer generate conscious thoughts about something or someone, we not only change that set of experiences out of which *we* act. We also change that set of experiences which *God* takes into consideration when determining which possibilities to present to us.

For illustrative purposes, let us again consider my prayer for my aunt. Assume that before my prayer, God wanted me to visit her. But let us further assume that God had not been attempting to persuade me to do so because God knew that in my current state of mind such attempts would have been useless. And finally, let us assume that after my prayer—after I have generated conscious thoughts about my aunt—God sees that divine persuasion may well have an effect and thus does attempt to lure me to visit.

Of course, given process thought, God cannot insure that such persuasion will be successful. But, in the words of David Griffin and John Cobb, such divine persuasion "is not ineffective."[17] In other words, all things being equal, I am more likely to visit my aunt if God is luring me to do so. Now let us suppose that primarily because of this luring, I do in fact decide to visit my aunt. We could then justifiably conclude that my prayer had efficaciously affected me. That is, we could justifiably claim that it was primarily because I prayed—thereby creating the conscious thoughts related to my aunt which in turn brought about God's efficacious luring—that I did finally visit her.

Given process thought, this concept of efficacy also seems acceptable. Again, however, qualification is necessary. Since this model of efficacy is based on the assumption that God cannot unilaterally cause us to do anything, it cannot be accepted by those classical theists who hold that God has specific sovereignty. But this is not necessarily the case for those classical theists who affirm general sovereignty. Unlike process theists, classical proponents of general sovereignty do believe that God has the *power* to cause us unilaterally to think or do anything. But they also believe, remember, that God has chosen as a general rule not to exercise such power in order to create a context in which we can make meaningful, free moral decisions and/or improve our relationship with the divine. In other words, it is perfectly compatible with this branch of classical thought to assume as a general rule that God is, as process theists contend, only attempting to persuade individuals to think and act in a manner consistent with the divine will. And given this fact, such classical theists, like process theists, can maintain that intercessory prayer is efficacious for the petitioner in the sense just outlined.

Second, the relationship between this type of efficacy and intercessory prayer is again somewhat accidental. What gives God the ability to lure us more effectively in this context is not the petition, itself, or even the fact that we are in a state of prayer. The basis for the efficacy is again the fact that conscious thoughts about someone or something have been generated. And, thus, since it is questionable whether intercessory prayer best accomplishes this end, it is also questionable whether the type of efficacy just outlined can serve as a primary reason for engaging in this practice.

Suchocki also believes, however, that intercessory prayer is efficacious for others—that is, for those for whom the intercession is sought. One form of such efficacy follows directly from what already has been argued. Suchocki, remember, believes that in prayer we change "the reality with which God works" and that "the reality of the world has a real effect upon which possibilities may efficaciously be given." It should not be surprising, therefore, that she sees such expanded possibilities referring not only to God's interaction with petitioners but also to God's interaction with those persons for whom the petitions are offered.[18]

To return to the scenario concerning my aunt, let us assume that although she would like to ask me to visit and that she would do so if 'urged' by God, God has not been luring her to invite me because God knows that I have been busy and probably would not come. But let us also assume that while praying for my aunt, I generate conscious thoughts about her welfare which make it much more likely that I will visit if asked and thus that God, for this reason, urges my aunt to call. Since in this case the divine lure presented to my aunt is primarily the result of my prayer, it can meaningfully be said that my prayer has efficaciously affected the life of another.

Efficacy of this type also seems acceptable. But the same qualifications mentioned above apply here. This type of efficacy is also available to the classical proponent of general sovereignty. And, again, it seems that this type of efficacy is best viewed as a beneficial, but accidental, consequence of intercessory petitioning and not as its primary purpose.

There is, however, yet another way in which Suchocki believes that our intercessory prayers affect others. When we pray, she maintains, we do not change only our own past. We also change the past—the set of occurrent events—for the persons cited in the prayer. Thus, since every person "in the world must unify [himself] in light of [his] total past," our prayers for another are of real, direct relevance for him. Even if this prayer "is not directly given to his awareness, it is effective for him."[19]

In terms of our scenario, the contention here seems to be that my prayers for my aunt will directly affect her. Her world—the total set of experiences out of which she makes her decisions or forms her perspectives on life—will be changed. It will now include my prayers. Therefore, since her decisions or perspectives are influenced by that total set of experiences out of which they are generated, my prayers will to some extent affect my aunt's life.

This type of alleged efficacy is more controversial than the others Suchocki cites. It seems correct to say that *all* prayers for others of which they are consciously aware will have some impact on them. If, for example, my aunt discovers that I am praying for her, she will surely be affected in some way. She may feel loved, respond in love or even feel embarrassed. But some effect will occur. In fact, it may even be the case that all prayers for others of which they are only subconsciously aware will have some impact.

Moreover, it seems true that *many* prayers for others of which they are not directly aware on either a conscious or subconscious level can directly affect them. For instance, praying for my aunt could lead me to consider the needs of the elderly more seriously. This in turn might lead me to write to a certain congresswoman who has demonstrated a sensitivity in this area, and this in turn might cause her to support a certain bill which, if passed, would benefit my aunt directly.

But does Suchocki really mean to argue that all prayers for others of which they are not aware will have some *direct and immediate* effect on how they "unify our experience"? Does she really mean to argue that when I secretly pray for a distant aunt thousands of miles away, this prayer immediately becomes "part of the relevant past" in the life of my aunt and thus will have some direct effect on how she "unifies her experiences"?

It appears she does. In discussing a prayer offered for a killer, she claims that "insofar as you send unmitigated feelings of hatred toward him, his own unification of himself must relate to these feelings of hatred. Insofar as you change your feelings from harm to good in prayer, you have changed the reality of his world."[20] And she seems to think this effect takes place immediately.

It is not clear to me, however, that process theists need (or even ought to) agree with this interpretation of Suchocki's comments. Process theology does, as Suchocki points out, believe in a "world of total interdependence" in the sense that "each actuality is inescapably related to all others."[21] But such interdependence can be understood as mediate and indirect as well as immediate and direct.

Even if we grant, though, that this last model of efficacy offered by Suchocki is coherent, qualification is again needed. First, if intercessory prayer does have this immediate, direct effect on others, then it does so for all those engaged in this activity, whether classical or process in persuasion. Second, such efficacy is again, at best, only tangentially related to prayer. What directly affects those for whom petitions are offered are the conscious thoughts generated while praying, thoughts which could be generated in many other ways. So, again, it does not appear that a primary reason for such prayer has been identified.

What then are we to conclude about Suchocki's discussion of intercessory petitioning? She has, I believe, shown that such petitioning can justifiably be viewed as efficacious from a process perspective. While process theists cannot view petitionary prayer as initiating unilateral divine activity, they can rightly view such prayer as an activity which meaningfully affects the petitioner, God and those for whom intercession is being sought. However, Suchocki has not shown that "the distinctive way in which process thought formulates the relationship betwen God and the world provides a new frame of reference for considering the dynamics of prayer," one that "promises a revitalization of prayer in that... with this renewal, prayer gains a clarity and simplicity which enhances its practice."[22] For she has not demonstrated that the process petitioner can generate any type of efficacy which cannot also be generated in the same fashion by the classical petitioner who affirms general sovereignty.

Moreover, and more importantly, Suchocki has not convincingly argued that intercessory petitioning is an *important* activity in which process theists should engage with *regularity*. For many classical proponents of general sovereignty, petitioning is important because, in addition to being seen as efficacious in the ways Suchocki outlines, it is also believed to be a method for initiating unilateral divine intervention. But all of the types of efficacy open to process theism flow entirely from the generation of certain conscious thoughts. And, as I have repeatedly pointed out, prayer is not required to generate such thoughts and is possibly not even the best method of doing so. Hence, in the last analysis,

Suchocki's discussion leaves us with a perplexing question: Even granting that petitionary prayer of certain types is efficacious, why should process theists feel any need to participate in this activity? Or, to state this question in terms of Pittenger's claim that petitionary prayer is not "absurd or irrelevant," even if it is granted that such prayer is not absurd, why should it be seen as relevant?[23]

It is important not to confuse this question with the question of whether process theists have a sound basis for regularly engaging in conscious prayer at all. To this latter question process theists such as Suchocki, Pittenger and Mason have a ready reply, one that is similar to that offered by many classical theists. God, they argue, is not only with us in every moment in an active and receptive way. God is also, in the words of Mason, " the *personal* center of the universe." Thus, "our relationship with God should always be a personal one." But just as meaningful, growing personal relationships on the human level require "intense, conscious discussions," so it is with God. "For our relationship with God to be enhanced we need to stop occasionally and attempt to put it into sharper, more conscious focus. We need consciously to air our needs, our desires and hopes for the world and for ourselves, our grievances and our delights and those things for which we are thankful."[24]

It seems to me that, as a justification for conscious prayer, such a 'relational' argument is compelling. But it is difficult to see how this line of reasoning could in any sense help justify the practice of *petitionary* prayer within the process system. In fact, it seems to me that just the opposite is true. We do need to interact personally with friends to maintain relationships. And such interaction does presuppose that both parties share one another's burdens and desire to meet one another's needs. Moreover, such interaction may well include petitioning—that is, may include asking one's friends for assistance or intercession. But let us suppose that a friend tells us that she is already doing all that can be done in a given situation. We would then no longer continue to ask for her assistance. It would, in fact, be an insult to do so.

The same, it seems to me, holds for the relationship between God and the process theist. The process theist may well need to interact with (communicate with, share with) God in order to maintain a vital personal relationship. She may need to air her needs, desires and hopes. But as has been repeatedly emphasized, the God of process theism cannot unilateraly intervene to heal a person or stop a crazed killer or even soothe an anxious mind. God does, of course, present all entities with the optimum real possibilities open to them and also attempts to persuade them to actualize such possibilities to the extent possible. But God is already doing so to the greatest extent possible. Thus, what possible basis can the process theist have for petitioning (asking, requesting) divine involvement in any literal sense? Does not such prayer, rather, actually reflect either ignorance of, or a lack of faith in, God's integrity?

But why be so literalistic, it might be argued. Of course process theists ought not petition God—request things from God—in the literal sense done by many classical theists. But as long as process theists understand what they are really saying when they use classical petitionary language, no real harm is done. For example, as long as they understand that when they ask God to give them peace or give world leaders wisdom or grant healing to a loved one, they are not really asking God to intervene unilaterally or do more than is already being done but are really only generating efficacious conscious thoughts, the use of such classical language is innocuous. In fact, since such language is so well ingrained in our Western religious tradition, it may be advantageous on both the personal and corporate level to continue its use.

I do not believe that such a response is open to process theists. In almost all contexts, process theists take great care to distinguish their view of God's relationship with the world from that affirmed by classical theists. With respect to the problem of evil, for example, they continually emphasize the fact that while the God of classical theism may choose at times not to intervene unilaterally, the God of process theism can *never* do so.

Accordingly, one must wonder why any process theist would want to allow such a blurring of this distinction in relation to prayer. This is especially true when we consider the fact that, for most people, religious terms derive their primary meaning from the meaning such terms commonly have in nonreligious (standard human) contexts. Thus, since to petition on the human level is to ask someone to do something which may not otherwise be done, this 'inaccurate' concept of petitioning is likely to be carried over into the religious realm for many, regardless of disclaimers process theists might make.

Conclusion

In closing, let me summarize what has, and has not, been argued. I have not argued that the classical models of petitionary prayer are nonproblematic. Classical proponents of specific sovereignty believe that divine activity is never in any sense dependent on human activity. Thus, it is questionable whether prayer within this model actually 'changes things' to any greater degree than it does within its process counterpart.

Classical proponents of general sovereignty (classical free will theists) do, on the other hand, affirm a model of prayer in which it can be said that God brings about certain states of affairs because humans have requested such intervention. However, the relationship between this model of prayer and the classical free will response to evil generates a dilemma. In response to the problem of evil, classical free will theists basically argue that, although God possesses the power to intervene in earthly affairs at will, God's creative agenda dictates that this power be used very sparingly, if at all. But if this is so,then it appears that such theists should also expect God to intervene in response to petitions sparingly, if at all. Here, it is the classical free will theist who cannot have it both ways.[25]

However, I have argued that the process model of petitionary prayer does generate serious, and to some extent unique, problems. Process theists do have a sound basis for regularly engaging in prayer. But since the God of process theism cannot unilaterally intervene and is already doing all that can be done, it makes no sense for process theists to literally petition God (ask God) for anything. Process theists, accordingly, must portray petitionary prayer in nonliteral terms—that is, as an activity in which we generate efficacious conscious thoughts by talking *with* God *about* things. But when this is done, it is no longer clear that prayer, as opposed to other methods of generating conscious thoughts, is the best way to generate such efficacy. Moreover, the continuing use of classical petitionary language blurs the important distinction which process theists see between their view of divine power and that held by classical theists. Accordingly, it seems to me that while classical theists must be very careful when discussing petitionary prayer, it would be best for process theists[26] to disavow petitionary prayer altogether.[27]

Chapter VI

GOD'S WILL

CAN IT BE CLEARLY DISCERNED IN THE PROCESS SYSTEM?

All Christians, we saw in Chapter V, believe it is important to pray. That is, they desire to share their thoughts and concerns with God. But most also want God to share the divine perspective with them. That is, most Christians sincerely want to know God's will.

To say that someone is seeking to know God's will can mean at least two things. It sometimes means that the person in question simply desires a better personal understanding of God's perspective on a given state of affairs. She might want to know, for example, whether her present manner of living is consistent with God's general goals for her life. Or she might want to know whether a certain person would be a good spouse. Or she might want to better understand God's perspective on pornography or foreign policy issues.

Sometimes, however, a person is seeking (or also seeking) to know how to act, given God's perspective on a given issue. For example, if a person comes to believe that her current manner of living is not consistent with God's ideal life-plan, she might also desire to know how God believes she can best begin to move toward this goal. Or, if she comes to believe that a given individual would be a good spouse, she might also want to know how God believes she can best help this person also arrive at this decision. Or, if she comes to believe that certain material is distasteful from

God's perspective, she might also desire to know if God wants her to try to make the production of such material illegal.

But, in either case, the same fundamental question arises: To what extent is it possible for believers to discern clearly God's will?[1] The purpose of this final chapter is to compare the classical and process[2] responses to this question. I shall conclude that, although classical theists[3] necessarily encounter a certain degree of difficulty when attempting to discern God's will, certain fundamental tenets in the process system—certain basic presuppositions about how God relates to the world—make the attainment of this goal much more difficult for process theists.

Process Perspective on Spiritual Discernment

Most classical theists believe that a clear conscious understanding of God's will is, in principle, attainable. They often differ on the means by which they believe such knowledge is best attained. Some say God's will is primarily to be found in the Bible. Others turn primarily to church tradition or some individual believed to be God's spokesperson. Still others primarily search for an 'inner light' or attempt to deduce God's specific will from general principles already held to be true. Of course, all classical theists acknowledge that such discernment is difficult, whatever techniques or combinations thereof are used. But most believe that such guidance is to some extent available to all. If one is open and diligent, one can, at times, come to a fairly clear, conscious understanding of what God believes or how God would have one act.

Most process theists disagree. The God of process theism, as we have seen, is always attempting to lure us to act in the best available manner. But "this process," John Cobb tells us, "is most of the time below the level of consciousness or at its fringes. Clear conscious decisions in relation to clear conscious knowledge of possibilities is a rare phenomenon."[4] Lewis Ford is even more emphatic:

> Consciousness emerges for complex actualities only in the later phases of experience, whereas the [divine] aim is operative from the first. There is plenty of opportunity for the

> aim to be completely distorted by the time it reaches consciousness. Only the very pure in heart can hear God aright.[5]

But if the goal of spiritual discernment is not to achieve a clear conscious understanding of the divine aim, what then should we seek? What should be sought, according to Cobb, is alignment "with God's purposes." We may not be able "to achieve a propositional knowledge of what those purposes are." However, we can act in such a way that our subconscious thoughts are more likely to be in tune with God's thoughts—that is, we can act in such a way that we will *be* more Godly in nature. And those who are subconsciously aligned with God, of course, are much more likely to *do* God's will, which is often the ultimate end sought.[6]

But how is such a subconscious state brought about? What are we to do to align ourselves subconsciously with God's purposes? The most important thing to keep in mind, Cobb states, is that 'God's will' is not something external to us which must be 'found' or 'discovered', even at the subconscious level. God's purposes are always automatically being presented to our subconscious to the greatest extent possible.

However, Cobb continues, "there is no reason to suppose that the aim derived from God will be stronger than the clamorous demands of the other factors that form [our] experience." That is, there is no reason to believe that just because we are always subconsciously aware of God's aims, we will always align ourselves with them. Accordingly, "our task is to free ourselves from the power of those forces that inhibit our alignment of ourselves with the divine aim which is toward growth in ourselves and others."[7]

What are such inhibiting forces? One of the main ones, we learn, is "the projection of our own past purposes." All of us have developed patterns of living that have worked for us in the past, that have helped us achieve desired goals. But what worked in the past may not be the best response in the changed circumstances of the present. Hence, "one needs constantly to check oneself to see whether one is allowing the actual situations to direct one's fresh response rather than imposing upon that response those patterns of the past."[8]

This means, among other things, Cobb points out, that we must avoid trying to deduce God's aim from general principles, even principles which we believe reflected God's aim for the past. God is continuously striving to maximize harmonious intensity—that is, to infuse novelty into his co-creation. Thus, if we desire to remain aligned with God's aims, we must always be willing to move beyond the status quo. We must "become more open to the unpredicatable call of God" and be willing to have it repeatedly transform our lives.[9]

The other major inhibiting force is said to be "the tension between our narrow interests and perceptions and God's aim at the more inclusive realization contributing to a more inclusive future." But this, too, can be overcome. If we practice loving our neighbors—"spend time empathetically entering into the life, the feelings, the needs, and the hopes of other persons and consciously willing their good"—we can bridge the gap between spiritual duty and personal desire. Or, as Cobb states this point in another context, we can by the exercise of love "so broaden our concerns as to reduce the debilitating effects of anxiety about our individual features without reducing a constructive concern about the future in general."[10]

Will this effort be of practical worth? Will the work required to overcome such inhibiting factors be useful in our daily lives? Yes, responds Cobb. To the extent one faces life with a spirit of loving openness, "one's purpose will blend with that of God. One can act beyond one's own understanding."[11]

Critique of the Process Perspective

There is one sense in which this model of spiritual discernment is rather noncontroversial. All Christians desire to align themselves with God's general purposes. That is, all desire to develop Godly dispositions and character. And all will agree that exercising a loving attitude and being open to God's novel subconscious leading are necessary if this end is to be achieved.

But how exactly is this model of subconscious spiritual growth to help us consciously respond to the vast array of perplexing, sometimes controversial, issues we continuously face on both the personal and corporate level? Would a specific career change better align us with God's general will for our lives? Ought we give up an unfulfilling job, even if the family suffers? Should we stay with our spouses for the sake of the children, no matter how unpleasant the relationship? Should we be working for a unilateral nuclear weapons freeze, or must we build more weapons to deter the Russians? Is capital punishment desirable in some cases? If so, which? Which poses the greatest threat to world peace: Marxist socialism or capitalistic totalitarianism? Is abortion ever justified? If so, when? Should we encourage, limit or stop genetic engineering?

"One cannot," Cobb has told us, "deduce...what needs to be done" in specific situations. But to the extent we have aligned ourselves with God's purposes, we will to some degree become subconsciously aware of how God wants us to respond to specific private and public issues. And although our conscious understanding of such guidance will "by no means purely [express] God's aim," we should trust this "sense of rightness" as being grounded in God's presence within us and act upon it.[12]

Such a response, however, generates a perplexing question which must be faced by proponents of any subjective model of spiritual guidance: Since our own personal and cultural biases are often extremely hard to detect, let alone eradicate, how can we be sure that any given *conscious* "sense of rightness" is really grounded in God? Or, if we assume that bias can never be completely eliminated, the question becomes: How do we determine to what extent a given conscious "sense of rightness" is a reflection of God's will and to what extent it is the product of self-concern or cultural interference?

Cobb attempts to ameliorate this difficulty to some degree by cautioning that we should not affirm our "impulses, inclinations, images, and hunches" in a totally uncritical fashion. Psychology, traditional religious experience and the advice of others can aid us in "understanding the sources of our impulses." However, he is quick to add that the *major* way in which we learn to conform more fully with the highest possibilities for our lives is not through what is received consciously from without. "Finally each stands alone listening for what she or he is called to do."[13]

Thus, the difficulty to a great extent still remains. When one finally "stands alone listening," how does one determine to what extent one's conscious "impulses, inclinations, images and hunches" are accurate reflections of God's will?

Classical subjectivists, as I have already implicitly mentioned, have a ready response. God can and does at times, they argue, allow us to intuit clear, conscious knowledge of the divine will. That is, God can and does at times override personal and cultural bias. Of course, we will not be able to prove to others that this has in fact occurred in any given situation. But there are some cases in which we ourselves have the deep conviction that this has occurred, and in such cases we can justifiably maintain that God's will has clearly been discerned.

Such a response, of course, is not open to the process subjectivist since the process system, in general, does not allow for the direct divine infusion of clear, propositional guidance at the conscious level. God almost always communicates with us clearly only at the subconscious level. Such communication might on rare occasions reach the consciousness intact. But there is no mechanism within the process system for determining when this has occurred. Thus, at the conscious level, the process subjectivist must always assume that he or she has intuited a somewhat distorted or incomplete understanding of what God would have him or her do.

Moreover, this is of practical significance. Assume that a process subjectivist comes to 'feel' consciously that accepting a proposal for marriage is God's will. Which aspect of this "sense of rightness" is it that "by no means purely expresses God's aim"? Has God really communicated to this person's subconscious that she is to marry the individual in question or only that she is to remain friends with him? Or assume that a process subjectivist consciously 'feels' that capital punishment is only justified when a police officer has been murdered. Which aspect of this "sense of rightness" is it that "by no means purely expresses God's aim"? Is the subconscious really aware of the fact that God desires no capital punishment or that God also favors capital punishment when a person already in prison for life commits a murder? What if the process subjectivist consciously 'feels' abortion to be justifiable only in the case of rape. What aspect of this "sense of rightness" probably fails to clearly express God's aim? And how is the process theist to know?

Now, of course, process theists have a perfect right to claim—as Cobb does—that in all such cases more than 'feelings' alone must be considered. But that is beside the point. The point is that to the extent to which process theists desire to utilize God's direct leading, they encounter a serious epistemological problem not faced by their classical counterparts. Since process theists, unlike classical theists, claim that clear, direct guidance from God occurs almost exclusively at the subconscious level, they can, in principle, have much less assurance than classical theists that their conscious sense of God's leading can be trusted, even if they are convinced that they are subconsciously aligned with God's will to the greatest extent humanly possible.

However, do most process theists really affirm the radically subjective model of guidance set forth by Cobb? Do they really believe that conscious reasoning has little or no importance in determining God's will? I think not. They do appear to agree with Cobb that spiritual discernment must start with a subjective openness to God's leading. And most seem to agree with Cobb that the "impulses, inclinations, images, and hunches we [consciously] experience when in an attitude of love and receptive openness" must be taken seriously.[14] In fact, it is doubtful that many process theists would affirm a course of action that goes against their most basic "sense of rightness," no matter how logical it might seem.

But, clearly, most process theists also believe it is *necessary* to subject their "impulses, inclinations, images, and hunches" to rigorous rational assessment in light of the process doctrine of God. In fact, it often appears that the *primary* purpose of many process discussions of current socio-political issues is to determine which of the competing subjective perspectives has the greatest rational support. For example, in his discussion of liberation theology, David Griffin argues that the primary reason process theists must work for a better society is that such activity follows from the process conception of God.[15]

Even Cobb, himself, in a separate discussion on the role of the process theist in the contemporary cultural arena, agrees that the process theist's socio-political activity must be rationally grounded in the process understanding of the relationship between God and the world. In fact, he concludes at one point that "process theists have no way to escape [the] need for calculative reflection and all the ambiguities it introduces."[16]

In short, although, it is true that process theists take "impulses, inclinations, images and hunches" seriously, it seems undeniable that objective, rational, propositional reasoning must *also* be seen as a necessary component in most process models of spiritual discernment.

But to the extent this is true, a basic difficulty again arises. This problem—which I shall call the problem of finite perspective—must be faced to some extent by *any* theist who attempts to deduce specific activity from (or evaluate specific activity in light of) general principles believed to be sanctioned by God. Take, for example, the biblical mandate that we love one another. All Christians accept this principle as normative. But what exactly is the most loving course of action in any given situation—that is, which possible action will produce what is 'best' for the recipient of our love? Is it most loving to spank or to refrain from spanking our recalcitrant children? Is it most loving to support verifiable bilateral nuclear deterrence or unilateral disarmament? Is it most loving to divorce or attempt reconcilation? The problem, of course, is that we as humans are seldom able to identify clearly all the relevant variables and usually even less able to predict future consequences. Thus, such 'deductions' or assessments are for all theists always somewhat of a gamble.

But this problem acquires a whole new dimension of complexity within the process system. The basis for such complexity lies in the radically nonanthropocentric nature of most process thought. In classical thought there is certainly no pretense of understanding all of God's creative goals. But as process theists, themselves, often point out, classical theists do clearly believe that humanity is the primary focus of God's creative activity. The rest of creation is seen as important; it is sometimes even seen as having a great deal of intrinsic value. And although it is held that humanity has been given control over the rest of creation, it is also believed that such power is not to be abused. The natural environment and the rest of the animal kingdom should be the objects of good stewardship. But God's most fundamental creative goal in classical thought is clear. It is to create a context in which *humans* can come to love God with all their hearts and love their neighbors as themselves. Or, stated differently, God's most fundamental creative goal is held to be the spiritual and social well-being of humans.

However, as I first stated in Chapter IV, this is clearly not the ultimate creative goal for the God of process theism. God's ultimate goal is the greatest possible degree of harmonious intensity. And, as Ford has put it, it is quite conceivable that God's attempts to achieve this end might cause the evolutionary process to "bypass man and the entire class of mammals to favor some very different species capable of greater complexity than man can achieve."[17] In short, in process thought humans clearly lose the special status they possess in classical thought. And this, not surprisingly, has important, practical implications for the problem of 'finite perspective'—the problem of trying to deduce specific activity from a general principle without the capacity for identifying or predicting all the relevant factors.

Let us consider, for instance, our recently acquired ability to manipulate the basic genetic structure of cells. Ought the Christian oppose this practice? Or should it, if sanctioned, at least have certain limitations imposed? What causes the classical theist problems in this context is not the ultimate divine principle upon which her response should be based. That is *clear.* Our mandate is to help foster the spiritual and social betterment of humanity. What is somewhat *unclear* is exactly how this is to be accomplished in the context at hand.

However, as just stated, the welfare of humanity is not the highest creative goal from a process perspective. Of course, the God of process theism wants every entity to have a maximally enjoyable existence. Thus, God certainly does not want to generate unnecessary danger for the human species. But God's ultimate goal is an increase in harmonious intensity, and this always entails genuine risks for those who benefit most from the *status quo.*

Accordingly, might it not be the case that the God of process theism would welcome the development of genetic engineering, even if God believed that such engineering *could* well lead to severe problems for (even the subjugation or extinction of) the human race? Might not God see the risk worth the price? I do not know. But it would appear that such questions—questions about the relevant divine principles themselves—are the ones with which thoughtful process theists must grapple before questions concerning the practical application of this technology can even be considered.

Or, let us consider the sometimes uneasy relationship between humanity and the rest of the animal kingdom. Does God, as a general rule, presently give preference to humanity? Does God, for example, desire humans to kill malarial mosquitoes with which they must come into contact?

Within the classical system, the answer is, in principle, rather straightforward. We ought not treat the life of God's creatures lightly. And, of course, we must make sure that we have our facts straight. Are the mosquitoes in question really carrying malaria? Is it necessary to come in contact with them? What might be the negative environmental impact of exterminating all the mosquitoes in a given area? But the relevant principle is clear: If the choice is really between human life and the life of a malarial mosquito, then, all other things being equal, human life is to be given preference.

The process response is less clear. At one point, Cobb argues that we might

> expect that God would lure each entity toward that activity maximally beneficial to other entities, and that the entities chiefly considered would be those capable of the greatest realization of value. For example, one would judge that God would seek to persuade a malarial mosquito to starve rather than to feed upon a human being. But there is no evidence of such an activity on God's part.[18]

But why? Why doesn't God give preference to humans in this way? One reason, Cobb informs us, is that "God seems to call every living thing to a self-actualization in which immediate satisfaction looms large ... even at the price of endangering harmony and order."[19]

But in a different context Cobb and Griffin offer a seemingly conflicting response. We can "justify killing a malarial mosquito ... to save human life" because "there is nothing in the process view to suggest that we should have equal reverence for all actualities, even all living ones.... Everything else being equal those with the greater intrinsic value are to be preferred."[20]

Which way is it? When adjudicating such conflicts, does God generally favor those entities with greater intrinsic value at the expense of 'self-actualization' for all? Or does God favor 'self-actualization' for all, even though this may be disadvantageous to those entities with greater intrinsic value? Is our perspective to be the same as God's in this context? Or is it not necessary that we should have equal reverence for all life, even though God, as Ford puts its, must be "perfectly partial to all"?[21]

I do not wish to claim that answers to such questions are not available. However, I do not believe they are obvious within the process system. But this again simply exemplifies the fact that many process theists face a serious second-level problem related to our finite perspective. Not only must they, along with classical theists, struggle to determine with accuracy exactly how specific activities will impact the well-being of humanity; they must also grapple with the most fundamental of all the relevant principles in the socio-political context—the role of humanity vis-à-vis God's ultimate creative aim—in a way in which classical theists need not. Or, to state this tension in a slightly different manner yet, while both classical and process theists are often unclear on exactly what follows from general beliefs about God's aims, process theists also face significant ambiguities related to the fundamental status of humanity, itself, within such aims.

It appears at times that process theists recognize this fact. Cobb and Griffin, for example, at one point state the following:

> As long as we try to solve the [problem of discerning what is right] through our rational and calculative procedures, tensions remain, for we cannot calculate the relative importance of morality and adventure, and there is no assurance that the results of our best calculations will coincide with God's aims. God's aim is in terms of the inclusive reality beyond the possibility of our minds to fathom.[22]

This may be why process theists at times are so desirous to make discernment a subconscious, subjective matter. But most process theists *do* at times engage in rational, calculative discussions concerning God's will. And to the extent this is done, they face the problem of finite perspective just outlined.

Conclusion

What we find then, in the last analysis, is that many process theists encounter a serious double-barreled epistemological challenge when attempting to discern God's will. In one sense, this is nothing unusual. Classical theists, as we have seen, also face significant epistemological challenges. But the problems facing process theists are, in principle, more serious.

To the extent that any theist bases spiritual discernment on subjective experience, the verification problem arises: How is one to know that one's 'sense of leading' has actually come from God? But while classical theists maintain that the assurance that one has received clear, conscious, propositional divine input is actually possible for all, process theists deny this. They maintain rather that subjective discernment will seldom, if ever, furnish direct divine guidance; it is almost always subject to some degree of conscious distortion. Or as Cobb puts it, a conscious sense of God's leading "can by no means purely express God's aim."[23]

On the other hand, to the extent that any theist bases spiritual discernment on rational calculation, the problem of finite perspective arises: How can we, as finite humans, identify all the relevant factors necessary to deduce appropriate responses to specific problems from the general doctrinal principles we believe to be relevant? But while classical theists at least have a clear idea as to the ultimate goal at which our specific behavior should be directed, such does not appear to be the case for process theists. The fact that the spiritual and social betterment of humanity is not God's ultimate creative goal makes "God's aim," in the words of Cobb and Griffin, "beyond the possibility of our minds to fathom."[24]

Such problems, of course, do not stand as a valid classical *criticism* of the process system. That is, such problems do not alone demonstrate that the classical model of discernment is superior to (more adequate than) its process counterpart. To establish this, one would need to establish that God actually can clearly communicate with humans at the conscious level and/or does actually hold humanity to be the ultimate creative goal. And this I have not attempted to demonstrate. I have in this chapter, rather, used the classical model primarily as a comparative tool, one which allows us to identify more clearly the necessary implications of the process perspective on divine power for the process model of spiritual discernment.

Nor does it follow from anything I have said that process theists should not attempt to discover God's will for their lives or involve themselves in discussions on current socio-political issues. As concerned Christians, they have a duty to attempt to live Godly lives and help resolve the perplexing cultural problems which cause so much mental and physical anguish for so many. But it would appear that, given the *very* tentative link between their best conscious thoughts and God's actual perspective on any specific issue, process theists,[25] *qua* process theists, should be *very* reluctant to endorse strongly any specific sense of leading (or 'solution') as the one God actually sanctions. A spirit of tentativeness would seem more appropriate.

EPILOGUE

In each chapter, I have argued that the Whiteheadian/ Hartshornean conceptualization of God's power generates specific problems. In closing, it may be helpful to paint in broader thematic strokes what I see the fundamental problem—and thus the most fundamental task for the process theist—to be.

I believe the key metaphysical linchpin in the process theological system is the contention that God cannot unilaterally bring about any actual state of affairs. It is the foundation on which most process theists build their positions on issues such as human coercion, evil, eschatology, prayer and divine guidance. And it is the basis for most attempts to demonstrate that the process perspective on such topics is superior to that held by classical Christian thinkers.

I have argued, however, that this 'metaphysical linchpin' is not a sound foundation for either effort. First, I have suggested that, although process theists can justifiably contend that the process system *does* not allow for coercive activity on God's part, they have failed to demonstrate that a being with the acknowledged powers of the God of process theism *could* not coerce. If this is true, then of course the process perspective on all the issues we have discussed will need to be rethought.

But more importantly, I have argued that, even if the God of process theism cannot coerce, little of moral import—and thus little of comparative value—follows. It does follow from the fact that the God of process theism cannot coerce that this being cannot unilaterally insure the occurrence of less evil or unilaterally intervene in response to petitionary prayer or insure that good will ultimately triumph or insure that the 'scales will be balanced' in an afterlife or give us direct, conscious guidance. But it does not follow from the fact that the God of process theism cannot coerce that the God of classical theism, who can unilaterally intervene (coerce) in all the ways just mentioned, ought to do so to any greater or lesser degree in any given context. For process theists to make this type of normative judgment, which they frequently do, they must determine whether the God of process theism would exert such coercive control if this were an option. That is, process theists must decide God's moral perspective on coercion.

As we have seen, however, it is not clear that many process theists have yet done so. At times, it appears that most believe that any divine coercive activity would be morally wrong or at least morally inferior. Most contend, for instance, that only purely persuasive power is perfect or generates the most worthwhile results. Others contend that the assurance of ultimate victory over evil found in classical thought destroys or minimizes the need for faith in God and our desire to help those presently in need. And some even contend that direct, conscious divine guidance is too coercive to be compatible with true self-determination.

At other times, however, many (often the same) process theists appear to believe that the God of process theism would coerce if this were possible or at least that coercion is morally superior to noncoercion in some cases. Many contend, for instance, that a being who could coercively remove more evil ought to do so. Many also contend that human coercion—even violent coercion—is at times required. And at least some seen to believe that it would be good if the righteous could receive just recompense in an afterlife.

It is this sort of equivocation or ambiguity which I believe to be at the heart of the majority of the problems I have raised in this book. Accordingly, what I see as the most important task for process theists at present should be clear. They need to develop a much more comprehensive understanding of the *moral* status of coercive power within the process system. Such an effort would not resolve all the problems at hand. But it would go a long way toward creating a foundation on which process theists could more firmly ground their moral assessment of the God of classical theism and their beliefs about proper human behavior.

In closing, one additional comment is necessary. I have argued throughout not only that classical free will Christianity (and to a lesser extent classical Christianity in general) can successfully defend itself against the process attacks we have considered but also that the classical responses (especially the classical free will responses) to the issues in question are every bit as plausible as those offered by process thought.

But, even if I am correct, this alone does not demonstrate that any variant of classical theism is actually superior to—or even on a metaphysical par with—process thought. For I have not discussed *all* the issues relevant to such an overall comparative assessment. I have not, for instance, adequately compared the concept of the identity of the self in each. And I have not (in this context) discussed many of the allegedly inconsistent aspects of classical thought—for example, the problematic relationship between divine foreknowledge and human freedom. Thus, all that *directly* follows in a comparative sense from what I have argued is that the various process arguments with which I have concerned myself in this book do not demonstrate the process theological system to be superior to that found in classical Christianity, especially its free will variant.

NOTES

Introduction

1. Norman Pittenger, "Process Thought as a Conceptuality for Reinterpreting Christian Faith," *Encounter* 44 (1983): 109; George Shields, "God, Modality and Incoherence," *Encounter* 44 (1983): 27.

2. F. Duane Lindsey, "An Evangelical Overview of Process Theology," *Bibliotheca Sacra* (January-March, 1977): 15.

3. R. C. Sproul, "The Relativity Blitz and Process Theology," *Christianity Today* (April 23, 1982): 50.

4. Delwin Brown, Ralph James, Gene Reeves, eds., *Process Philosophy and Christian Thought* (New York: The Bobbs-Merrill Company, Inc., 1971), p. v.

5. A good summary of the literary history of the process tradition can be found in John B. Cobb and David Ray Griffin, *Process Theology: An Introductory Exposition* (Philadelphia: The Westminster Press, 1976), pp. 162-185.

6. Brown, James and Reeves, p. v.

7. Schubert Ogden shares much in common with the other leading proponents of the Whiteheadian/Hartshornean tradition. In fact, many discussions of process thought fail to note any significant divergence. However, with respect to the aspect of process thought with which this book is concerned—the process concept of divine power—Ogden believes he does differ from the others significantly. Specifically, he has informed me in private correspondence that, while many other process theists do claim that God attempts to 'persuade' other entities to actualize the divine ideal, his claim is only that God sets the optimum logical limits within which free choice can be made. Accordingly, at those points in the discussion where this distinction becomes significant, Ogden should be exempted from my critique.

8. I will not continue to state explicitly in the text that I am discussing the Whiteheadian/Hartshornean school of process thought. However, all occurrences of the phrases 'process system', 'process thought' and 'process theism' in this book should be read with this in mind.

9. Charles Hartshorne, *Man's Vision of God and the Logic of Theism* (Chicago: Willet, Clark, 1941), p. 185.

10. Hartshorne and Griffin maintain that God in no sense created the process. On the other hand, Ford, in keeping with Whitehead, believes that God nontemporally establishes the basic metaphysical principles and hence the basic structure of the process in question. See Lewis Ford, ed., *Two Process Philosophers: Hartshorne's Encounter With Whitehead* (American Academy of Religion, 1973), pp. 47ff., 67-72.

11. Cobb and Griffin, pp. 102-103.

12. This should not be taken to mean, of course, that process theists do not take the concept of the Incarnation, as they intepret it, seriously. See, for example, David Griffin, *A Process Christology* (Philadelphia: The Westminster Press, 1973).

13. Pittenger, p. 110.

14. Lindsey, p. 16.

15. Arthur Holmes, *Contours of a World-View* (Grand Rapids: Eerdmans, 1983), p. 77.

16. Lindsey, p. 15.

17. Royce Gruenler, *The Inexhaustible God* (Grand Rapids: Baker Book House, 1983), p. 7.

18. Lindsey, p. 26.

19. Bruce Demarest, *General Revelation* (Grand Rapids: Zondervan, 1982), p. 174.

20. Clark Pinnock, "Between Classical and Process Theism," in *Process Theology*, ed. by Ronald Nash (Grand Rapids: Baker Book House, 1987), p. 319.

21. Michael Peterson, "Orthodox Christianity, Wesleyanism, and Process Theology," *Wesleyan Journal* 15 (Fall, 1980): 54.

22. Harold B. Kuhn, "The Process Theology Word Game," *Christianity Today*, Oct. 8, 1982, p. 106.

23. David Burrell, "Does Process Theology Rest on a Mistake?" *Theological Studies* 43 (1982), pp. 132, 133.

24. Ronald Nash, "Process Theology and Classical Theism," in *Process Theology*, p. 22.

25. Gruenler, p. 30.

26. Cobb and Griffin, p. 9.

27. Langdon Gilkey, "A Theology in Process: Schubert Ogden's Developing Theology," *Interpretation* 21 (1967): 449.

28. Illtyd Trethowan, "The Signficance of Process Theology," *Religious Studies* 19: 318; W. Norris Clark, *The Philosophical Approach to God* (Winston-Salem, N.C.: Wake Forest University, 1979).

29. Trethowan, p. 314.

30. Burrell, p. 128.

31. Gruenler, p. 16.

32. Pinnock, p. 318.

33. Peterson, p. 52.

34. See, for example, David Mason, "Reflections on 'Prayer' from a Process Perspective," *Encounter* 45 (Autumn, 1984): 347-356.

35. Schubert Ogden, *Reality of God and Other Essays* (San Francisco: Harper & Row, 1966), p. 17.

36. Robert Neville, *Creativity and God: A Challenge to Process Theism* (New York: Seabury Press, 1980), p. 86.

37. Cobb and Griffin, p. 14.

38. William Craig, "Divine Foreknowlege and Future Contingency," in *Process Theology*, pp. 95-115.

39. Theodore Vitali, "Lewis S. Ford's Revision of Whitehead: God as the Future of All Occasions," *Encounter* 44 (1983): 18-19.

40. David Griffin, *God, Power and Evil: A Process Theodicy* (Philadelphia: Westminster Press, 1976), p. 276.

41. Gruenler, p. 35.

42. Griffin, p. 279.

43. Neville.

44. Lewis Ford, "Divine Persuasion and Coercion," *Encounter* 47 (Summer, 1986), pp. 268-269.

45. Lewis Ford, *The Lure of God* (Philadelphia: Fortress Press, 1978), p. 27; John B. Cobb, *God and the World* (Philadelphia: Westminster Press, 1976), p. 90.

46. Mason, p. 347.

47. Neville, pp. 116-136.

48. Burrell, p. 126.

Chapter I

1. For reasons given in the Introduction, I am assessing the views of only those process theists in the Whiteheadian/Hartshornean tradition. All occurrences of the phrases 'process theism' and 'process theists' in this book should be read with this in mind.

2. As stated in the Introduction, I will be comparing process theism with classical Christian thought of an Augustinian/Thomistic variety because this is the variety of classical theism with which process theists normally compare themselves.

3. See, for example, Barry Whitney, "Process Theism: Does a Persuasive God Coerce?" *The Southern Journal of Philosophy* 17 (1979), pp. 133-141.

4. Lewis Ford, "Divine Persuasion and the Triumph of Good," in

Process Philosophy and Christian Thought, eds. D. Brown, R. James, O. Reeves (New York: The Bobbs-Merrill Company, Inc., 1971), pp. 291, 295.

5. Daniel Day Williams, "How Does God Act in Whitehead's Metaphysics?" in *Essays in Process Theology*, ed. by Perry LeFevre (Chicago: Exploration Press, 1985), p. 113. See also Bernard Loomer, "Whitehead's Method of Empirical Analysis," in *Process Theology: Basic Writings*, ed. Ewert H. Cousins (New York: Newman Press, 1971), p. 80.

6. John Cobb, *God and the World* (Philadelphia: The Westminster Press, 1969), p. 91.

7. John B. Cobb and David Griffin, *Process Theology: An Introductory Exposition* (Philadelphia: The Westminster Press, 1976), p. 125.

8. Ford, p. 288.

9. Cobb and Griffin, p. 53.

10. Ford, p. 289.

11. David Griffin, *God, Power and Evil: A Process Theodicy* (Philadelphia: The Westminster Press, 1976), p. 281.

12. Ibid., p. 266.

13. Ibid.

14. Ibid., p. 267.

15. Since process theists believe that all actual entities possess some form of self-determination, analogous questions arise in relation to nonhuman aggregates.

16. Lewis Ford, "Divine Persuasion and Coercion" *Encounter 47* (Summer, 1986): 269. See also John B. Cobb, "Spiritual Discernment in a Whiteheadian Perspective," in *Religious Experience and Process Theology*, eds. Harry Cargas and Bernard Lee (New York: Paulist Press), pp. 360-61.

17. Cobb and Griffin, p. 102.

18. Cobb and Griffin, p. 71.

19. Griffin, p. 292.

20. Ibid., p. 282.

21. Ibid., p. 292.

22. Ibid.

23. Cobb and Griffin, p. 73.

24. Ibid., pp. 71, 72. Ford is not in total agreement at this point. See note 10, Introduction.

25. Griffin, p. 277.

26. See note 7, Introduction.

27. Much of the material in this chapter first appeared in the *Journal of Religion* 64 (July, 1984): 332-47. © 1984 by The University of Chicago.

Chapter II

1. See note 1, Chapter I.

2. Charles Hartshorne, *The Divine Relativity* (New Haven: Yale University Press, 1948), p. 154.

3. John B. Cobb and W. Widick Schroeder, eds., *Process Philosophy and Social Thought* (Center for the Scienfitic Study of Religion, 1981), p. 70.

4. John B. Cobb, *Process Theology as Political Theology* (Philadelphia: The Westminster Press, 1982), p. 106.

5. David Griffin, *God, Power and Evil* (Philadelphia: The Westminster Press, 1976), p. 326.

6. Cobb, pp. 92-108.

7. As stated in note 10, Introduction, Lewis Ford, unlike Cobb and Griffin, believes God did "have a hand" in the creation of the metaphysical principles which limit divine involvement in earthly affairs.

8. D. Brown, R. James, D. Reeves, eds., *Process Philosophy and Christian Thought* (New York: Bobbs-Merrill Co., 1971), p. 284; Lewis Ford, *The Lure of God* (Philadelphia: Fortress Press, 1978), p. 27.

9. John B. Cobb and David Griffin, *Process Theology: An Introductory Exposition* (Philadelphia: The Westminster Press, 1976), pp. 118f.

10. John B. Cobb, *God and the World* (Philadelphia: The Westminster Press, 1969), p. 90.

11. Hartshorne, p. 154.

12. This phrase actually refers to classical *Christian* theists. See note 2, Chapter I.

13. Cobb and Schroeder, p. 193.

14. Ford, p. 23.

15. Cobb, *God and the World*, pp. 20-41.

16. Cobb, *Process Theology as Political Theology*, p. 107.

17. Charles Hartshorne, *Man's Vision of God and the Logic of Theism* (Chicago: Willet, Clarke, 1941), p. 171; Hartshorne, *The Divine Relativity*, pp. 154-55.

18. Cobb and Schroeder, pp. 26-28.

19. Cobb, *Process Theology as Political Thought*, p. 107.

20. Cobb and Schroeder, p. 70.

21. Ibid., p. 107.

22. Cobb, *Process Theology as Political Thought*, p. 149.

23. Cobb and Schroeder, p. 195.

24. Hartshorne, *The Divine Relativity*, p. 154.

25. Lewis Ford, "Divine Persuasion and Coercion," *Encounter* 47 (Summer, 1986).

26. Ogden believes that humans desiring to do God's will might at times need to engage in violent coercion. But he holds that, rather than attempting to 'persuade' us, "God's only aim or intention in exercising his power is to...optimize the limits of [his creatures'] own free decisions by establishing such fundamental limits of natural order as to allow for a greater possibility of good than evil to be realized through their exercise of freedom," *Faith and Freedom* (Nashville: Abingdon Press, 1979), pp. 89-90, 94. Thus the critique of this chapter does not, strictly speaking, apply to his position on human coercion. But I believe that by focusing on the moral value he places on 'freedom', an analogous critique can be generated.

27. Much of the material in this chapter first appeared in *Process Studies* 15 (Fall, 1986): 161-171.

Chapter III

1. B.C. Johnson, "God and the Problem of Evil," in *Philosophy and Contemporary Issues*, ed. by J. Burr and M. Goldinger (New York: Macmillan, 1984), p. 127.

2. See note 1, Chapter I.

3. This phrase actually refers to classical Christian theism. See note 2, Chapter I.

4. Since some non-Christian theodicies are similar in structure to those found in classical Christian thought, my discussion of *classical* Christian theodicies may be of some use to those interested in the relationship between process theology and non-Christian religious thought on this issue.

5. Some process theists are primarily (or only) interested in pointing out that, from a process perspective, classical theodicies are incoherent because they are based on an incoherent concept of divine power. See, for example, Schubert Ogden, "Evil and Belief in God: The Distinctive Relevance of 'Process Theology'," *The Perkins School of Theology Journal*, 31 (Summer, 1978): 29-34.

6. David Griffin, *God, Power and Evil: A Process Theodicy* (Philadelphia: The Westminster Press, 1976), p. 270.

7. Ibid., p. 269ff.

8. Alvin Plantinga, *God, Freedom and Evil* (Grand Rapids: Eerdmans Publishing Company, 1977), pp. 165-89.

9. David Griffin and John Cobb, *Process Theology: An Introductory Exposition* (Philadelphia: The Westminster Press, 1976), p. 74.

10. Ibid., pp. 71-72, 74. Again, Lewis Ford differs somewhat from Griffin and Cobb at this point. He believes that God was to some extent involved in establishing the metaphysical principles in question. See note 10, Introduction.

11. See David Basinger, "Human Freedom and Divine Providence: Some New Thoughts on an Old Problem," *Religious Studies* 16 (1979): 500-01, 504.

12. Griffin and Cobb, p. 75.

13. Griffin, p. 271.

14. John Cobb, *God and the World* (Philadelphia: The Westminster Press, 1969), p. 90.

15. Basinger, pp. 503-04.

16. David Basinger and Randall Basinger, "Divine Omnipotence: Plantinga vs. Griffin," *Process Studies* 11 (Spring, 1981): 11-24.

17. F. R. Tennant, *Philosophical Theology*, Vol. 2 (Cambridge: The University Press, 1929), pp. 199ff.

18. Ibid., p. 201.

19. Ibid., p. 200.

20. Brian Hebblethwaite, *Evil, Suffering and Religion* (New York: Hawthorne Books, 1976), p. 73.

21. Bruce Reichenbach, "Natural Evils and Natural Laws: A Theodicy for Natural Evils," *International Philosophical Quarterly* 16 (June, 1976): 179-98.

22. Alvin Plantinga, "The Probabilistic Argument from Evil," *Philosophical Studies* 35 (January, 1979): 1-53.

23. See note 7, Introduction.

Chapter IV

1. See note 1, Chapter I.

2. John B. Cobb, Jr. and David Griffin, *Process Theology: An Introductory Exposition* (Philadelphia: The Westminster Press, 1976), pp. 118-19.

3. This phrase actually refers to classical *Christian* theism. See note 2, Chapter I.

4. See, for example, George Eldon Ladd, *A Theology of the New Testament* (Grand Rapids: Eerdmans Publishing Company, 1974).

5. Cobb and Griffin, p. 118.

6. Ibid.

7. Ibid., p. 117.

8. Lewis Ford, "Divine Persuasion and the Triumph of Good," in *Process Philosophy and Christian Thought*, eds. D. Brown, R. James, and O. Reeves (New York: Bobbs-Merrill Co., 1971), p. 297.

9. Ibid., pp. 297-98.

10. I do not mean to imply here that all process theists profess such 'faith'. But clearly some leading process thinkers do.

11. Ford, p. 298n.

12. Cobb and Griffin, pp. 13-29.

13. As mentioned before, Ford differs from Cobb and Griffin at this point. See note 10, Introduction.

14. David Griffin, *God, Power and Evil: A Process Theodicy* (Philadelphia: The Westminster Press, 1976), pp. 285-300.

15. Charles Hartshorne, *Omnipotence and other Theological Mistakes* (Albany: State University of New York Press, 1984), pp. 36-37.

16. Griffin, pp. 312-13.

17. John B. Cobb, Jr., *God and the World* (Philadelphia: The Westminster Press, 1969), p. 102.

18. Cobb, p. 102; Griffin, pp. 311-12.

19. Griffin, p. 312.

20. Cobb, p. 102.

21. Cobb and Griffin, pp. 119-120.

22. Ibid.

23. Ibid., p. 120.

24. Alfred North Whitehead, *Process and Reality* (New York: Macmillan, 1929), p. 517.

25. Cobb and Griffin, p. 120.

26. Hartshorne, p. 36.

27. Cobb, p. 99.

28. Ford, p. 300.

29. Ibid.; Griffin, pp. 302-03.

30. Griffin, pp. 303, 305.

31. Ford, p. 295.

32. Cobb, p. 95.

33. Ford, p. 290.

34. Cobb, p. 94.

35. Ibid. As I point out in Chapter VI, the interpretation of Cobb's comments are debatable in some respects. But such comments do keep us from assuming automatically that God *presently* gives preference to humans.

36. Ford, p. 298n.

37. Alfred North Whitehead, *Adventures of Ideas* (New York: The Macmillan Company, 1933), p. 367.

38. Ford, p. 304.
39. Griffin, p. 271.
40. Cobb and Griffin, p. 120.
41. Ibid., pp. 119-20.
42. Ibid., p. 120.
43. Ibid., p. 121.
44. Lewis Ford shared this comment in private correspondence.
45. See note 7, Introduction.

Chapter V

1. David Mason, "Reflections on 'Prayer' From a Process Perspective," *Encounter* 45 (Autumn, 1984): 347-48.

2. See note 1, Chapter 1.

3. This phrase actually refers to classical *Christian* theists. See note 2, Chapter I.

4. For a more detailed discussion of this concept, see David and Randall Basinger, *Predestination and Free Will* (Downer's Grove, Illinois: InterVarsity Press, 1986), pp. 7-99.

5. *Summa Theologiae*, 1A, q.19, a.8, r.2.

6. John Calvin, *Institutes of the Christian Religion*, trans. Henry Beveridge, II (Grand Rapids: Eerdmans Publishing Co., 1979), p. 147.

7. Martin Luther, *Martin Luther: Selections From His Writings*, ed. John Dillenberger (Garden City, New York: Anchor Books, 1961), p. 217.

8. See, for example, Mason, p. 348 and Norman Pittenger, *God's Way With Men* (London: Hodder and Stoughton, 1969), pp. 154-57.

9. For a more detailed discussion of this concept, see Basingers, pp. 99-177.

10. For a more detailed discussion of this perspective, see David Basinger, "Why Petition An Omnipotent, Omniscient, Wholly Good God?" *Religious Studies* 19 (1983), pp. 29-32.

11. For a more detailed discussion of this perspective, see David Basinger, *Religious Studies*, pp. 32-36.

12. Mason, p. 351.

13. Mason, pp. 351-52; Pittenger, pp. 154-60.

14. Pittenger, p. 156.

15. Marjorie Suchocki, "A Process Theology of Prayer," *American Journal of Theology and Philosophy* 2 (May, 1981): 39.

16. Suchocki, pp. 39, 40.

17. John B. Cobb and David Griffin. *Process Theology: An Introductory Exposition* (Philadelphia: The Westminster Press, 1976), p. 125.

18. Suchocki, pp. 39, 40.

19. Ibid., p. 39.
20. Ibid.
21. Ibid., pp. 34, 39.
22. Ibid., p. 33.
23. Suchocki is not the only process theist who has discussed the efficacy of intercessory prayer. Cobb and Ford have done so also. See Cobb, "Spiritual Discernment in a Whiteheadian Perspective," and Ford, "Our Prayers as God's Passions," in *Religious Experience and Process Theology*, eds. Harry Cargas and Bernard Lee (New York: Paulist Press, 1976), pp. 349-369, 429-438. But their reasoning is analogous to that found in Suchocki's discussion. Thus, I believe that these questions arise not just for Suchocki but for most process theists.
24. Mason, pp. 353-54.
25. For a fuller discussion of this point, see David Basinger and Randall Basinger, *Philosophy and Miracle* (Lewiston, NY: The Edwin Mellen Press, 1986), pp. 107-117.
26. See note 7, Introduction.
27. Much of the material in this chapter first appeared in the *Evangelical Journal* 4 (Fall, 1986): pp. 70-81.

Chapter VI

1. This question must not be confused with the question discussed in Chapter I: Does the God of process theism have the capacity to coerce? In that context I was asking whether the *subconscious* 'divine lure' could ever unilaterally control human behavior. Here I am discussing the extent to which a clear conscious understanding of the 'divine lure' is available to process theists.
2. See note 1, Chapter I.
3. This phrase actually refers to classical *Christian* theists. See note 2, Chapter I.
4. John B. Cobb, "Spiritual Discernment in a Whiteheadian Perspective," in *Religious Experience and Process Theology*, eds. Harry Cargas and Bernard Lee (New York: Paulist Press), pp. 360-61.
5. Lewis Ford, "Divine Persuasion and Coercion," *Encounter* 47 (Summer, 1986): 269.
6. Cobb, p. 361.
7. Ibid.
8. Ibid., p. 362.
9. Ibid., pp. 365, 367.
10. Ibid., pp. 364-65.
11. Ibid., p. 363.

12. Ibid., p. 362.

13. Ibid., p. 366.

14. Ibid., p. 365.

15. David Griffin, "Values, Evil, and Liberation Theology," in *Process Philosophy and Social Thought*, eds. John B. Cobb and W. Widick Schroeder (Center for the Scientific Study of Religion, 1981), pp. 190-196.

16. John B. Cobb, *Process Theology as Political Theology* (Philadelphia: The Westminster Press, 1982), p. 150.

17. Lewis Ford, "Divine Persuasion and the Triumph of the Good," in *Process Philosophy and Christian Thought*, eds. D. Brown, R. James, O. Reeves (New York: The Bobbs-Merrill Company, Inc., 1971), p. 290.

18. John B. Cobb, *God and the World* (Philadelphia: The Westminster Press, 1969), p. 94.

19. Ibid.

20. John B. Cobb and David Griffin, *Process Theology: An Introductory Exposition* (Philadelphia: The Westminster Press, 1976), p. 79.

21. Lewis Ford, "Our Prayers as God's Passions," in *Religious Experience and Process Theology*, p. 434.

22. Cobb and Griffin, p. 125.

23. Cobb, "Spiritual Discernment," p. 362.

24. Cobb and Griffin, p. 125.

25. See note 7, Introduction.

Bibliography

Basinger, David. "Why Petition an Omnipotent, Omniscient, Wholly Good God?" *Religious Studies* 19 (1983): 25-41.

Basinger, Randall. "Evangelicals and Process Theism: Seeking a Middle Ground." *Christian Scholar's Review* 15 (1986): 157-67.

Brown, Delwin, Ralph James, Gene Reeves, eds. *Process Philosophy and Christian Thought.* New York: Bobbs-Merrill Company, 1971.

Burrell, David B. "Does Process Theology Rest on a Mistake?" *Theological Studies* 43 (1982): 125-35.

Clarke, W. Norris, S. J. *The Philosophical Approach to God.* Winston-Salem: Wake Forest University Press, 1980.

Cobb, John B., Jr. *God and the World.* Philadelphia: The Westminster Press, 1969.

———*Process Theology as Political Theology.* Philadelphia: The Westminster Press, 1982.

———"Spiritual Discernment in a Whiteheadian Perspective," in *Religious Experience and Process Theology*, eds. Harry Cargas and Bernard Lee. New York: Paulist Press, 1976, pp. 349-368.

Cobb, John B., Jr. and David Griffin. *Process Theology: An Introductory Exposition.* Philadelphia: The Westminster Press, 1976.

Cousins, Ewert, ed. *Process Theology: Basic Writings.* New York: Newman, 1971.

Culp, John. "A Dialogue with the Process Theology of John Cobb, Jr." *Wesleyan Journal* 15 (Fall, 1980): 33-44.

Ford, Lewis. "Divine Persuasion and Coercion." *Encounter* 47 (Summer, 1986): 267-73.

———"Divine Persuasion and the Triumph of Good," in *Process Philosophy and Christian Thought*, eds. D. Brown, R. James, G. Reeves. New York: The Bobbs-Merrill Company, 1971, pp. 287-304.

———*The Lure of God*. Philadelphia: Fortress Press, 1978.

———"Our Prayers as God's Passions," in *Religious Experience and Process Theology*, pp. 429-438.

Frankenberry, Nancy. "Some Problems in Process Theodicy." *Religious Studies 18* (1982): 179-197.

Griffin, David. *God, Power and Evil: A Process Theodicy*. Philadelphia: The Westminster Press, 1976.

———"Values, Evil and Liberation Theology," in *Process Philosophy and Social Thought*, eds. John B. Cobb, Jr. and W. Widick Schroeder. Center for the Scientific Study of Religion, 1981.

Hartshorne, Charles. *The Divine Relativity*. New Haven: Yale University Press, 1948.

———*Omnipotence and Other Theological Mistakes*. Albany: State University of New York Press, 1984.

Hebblethwaite, Brian. *Evil, Suffering and Religion*. New York: Hawthorne Books, 1976.

Mason, David. "Reflections on 'Prayer' From a Process Perspective." *Encounter* 45 (Autumn, 1984): 347-356.

Mellert, Robert. *What is Process Theology?* New York: Paulist Press, 1975.

Nash, Ronald, ed. *Process Theology*. Grand Rapids: Baker Book House, 1987.

Neville, Robert. *Creativity and God*. New York: Seabury Press, 1980.

Ogden, Schubert. *Faith and Freedom: Toward a Theology of Liberation*. Nashville: Abingdon Press, 1979.

———"The Metaphysics of Faith and Justice." *Process Studies* 14 (Summer, 1985): 87-101.

Plantinga, Alvin. *God, Freedom and Evil*. Grand Rapids: Eerdmans, 1977, pp. 165-189.

Peters, Eugene. "Theology, Classical and Neo-Classical." *Encounter* 44 (1983): 7-15.

Peterson, Michael L. "Orthodox Christianity, Wesleyanism and Process Theology." *Wesleyan Journal* 15 (Fall, 1980): 45-58.

Pittenger, Norman. *Process Thought and Christian Faith.* New York: Macmillan, 1968.

Shafer, Susan S. "The Efficacy of Prayer in Process Thought." Unpublished manuscript, Colgate Rochester Divinity School, 1981.

Shields, George W. "God, Modality and Incoherence." *Encounter* 44 (1983): 27-39.

Suchocki, Marjorie. *God, Christ, Church: A Practical Guide to Process Theology.* New York: Crossroad, 1982.

Tennant, F. R. *Philosophical Theology*, Vol. 2. Cambridge: The University Press, 1929.

Trethowan, Illtyd. "The Significance of Process Theology," *Religious Studies* 19 (1983): 311-322.

Vitali, Theodore. "Lewis S. Ford's Revision of Whitehead: God as the Future of All Occasions." *Encounter* 44 (1983): 17-25.

Whitney, Barry. *Evil and the Process God.* Lewiston, NY: Edwin Mellen Press, 1985.

———"Process Theism: Does a Persuasive God Coerce?" *The Southern Journal of Philosophy* 17 (1979): 133-141.

INDEX